SPIRITUAL
ALCHEMY

Translation from the French
original title : L'ALCHIMIE SPIRITUELLE

Omraam Mikhaël Aïvanhov

SPIRITUAL ALCHEMY

2ⁿᵈ edition

Complete Works – Volume 2

EDITIONS PROSVETA

www.prosveta.com
international@prosveta.com

Editor-Distributor

Editions PROSVETA S.A. – B.P. 12 – 83601 Fréjus Cedex (France)

Distributors

AUSTRIA
MANDALA
Verlagsauslieferung für Esoterik
A-6094 Axams, Innsbruckstraße 7

BELGIUM
PROSVETA BENELUX
Van Putlei 105 B-2548 Lint
N.V. MAKLU Somersstraat 13-15
B-2000 Antwerpen
VANDER S.A.
Av. des Volontaires 321
B-1150 Bruxelles

BRAZIL
NOBEL SA
Rua da Balsa, 559
CEP 02910 - São Paulo, SP

BRITISH ISLES
PROSVETA Ltd
The Doves Nest
Duddleswell Uckfield,
East Sussex TN 22 3JJ
Trade orders to :
ELEMENT Books Ltd
Unit 25 Longmead Shaftesbury
Dorset SP7 8PL

CANADA
PROSVETA Inc.
1565 Montée Masson
Duvernay est, Laval, Que. H7E 4P2

GERMANY
PROSVETA DEUTSCHLAND
Höhenbergweg 14
D - Bad Tölz

HOLLAND
STICHTING
PROSVETA NEDERLAND
Zeestraat 50
2042 LC Zandvoort

HONG KONG
HELIOS – J. Ryan
P.O. BOX 8503
General Post Office, Hong Kong

IRELAND
PROSVETA IRL.
84 Irishtown – Clonmel

ITALY
PROSVETA Coop. a r.l.
Cas. post. 13046 – 20130 Milano

LUXEMBOURG
PROSVETA BENELUX
Van Putlei 105 B-2548 Lint

NORWAY
PROSVETA NORDEN
Postboks 5101
1501 Moss

PORTUGAL
PUBLICAÇÕES
EUROPA-AMERICA Ltd
Est Lisboa-Sintra KM 14
2726 Mem Martins Codex

SPAIN
ASOCIACIÓN PROSVETA ESPAÑOLA
C/ Ausias March n° 23 Principal
SP-08010 Barcelona

SWITZERLAND
PROSVETA
Société Coopérative
CH - 1808 Les Monts-de-Corsier

UNITED STATES
PROSVETA USA, Inc.—P.O. Box 1176
New Smyrna Beach, FL 32170-1176
Web : www.prosveta-usa.com
E-mail : sales@prosveta-usa.com
VENEZUELA
Betty Munóz Urbanización Los Corales - avenida Principal
Quinta La Guarapa - LA GUAIRA - Municipio Vargas

Editions Prosveta S.A. – B.P. 12 – 83601 Fréjus Cedex (France)

ISBN 2-85566-371-7

édition originale : ISBN 2-85566-331-8

*The reader will better understand certain aspects
of the lectures published in the present volume
if he bears in mind that Master Omraam Mikhaël Aïvanhov's
Teaching was exclusively oral.*

Omraam Mikhaël Aïvanhov

TABLE OF CONTENTS

Preamble 11

1 Gentleness and Humility 13

2 'Except Ye Die Ye Shall Not Live' 35

3 Living in Conscious Reciprocity with Nature 55

4 The Unjust Steward 73

5 Lay Up For Yourselves Treasures 103

6 The Miracle of the Loaves and Fishes 117

7 The Feet and the Solar Plexus 137

8 The Parable of the Tares 155

9 Spiritual Alchemy 181

10 Spiritual Galvanoplasty 201

11 The Mother's Role During Gestation 221

PREAMBLE

Those who seek the reality that lies beneath the surface, will find, here, the key to the great mysteries of the Cabbalah, Alchemy and Astrology.

When the Everlasting Lord had set up the four Cardinal points of the compass: North, South, East and West, He created the four elements: fire, air, water and earth, from which all things were made. He then ordered them thus: Fire, which is hot and dry was placed at the North, which is cold and wet. Water, which is cold and wet, was placed at the South, which is hot and dry. Air, hot and wet, was placed in the East, also hot and wet, thus serving as a link between fire and water, by drawing to itself the heat of fire and wetness of water. The Earth, cold and wet, took its place in the West which is also cold and wet. Earth, too, served to link fire and water and, at the same time, balanced air in the East. As earth lies below water, air and fire, it received energy from all three and was thus able to nourish all creatures.

When earth united with fire from the North, it produced gold (the alchemists' Sun); when it was joined to water it produced silver (the alchemists' Moon). When earth was joined to air which was united to fire and water, copper (the alchemists' Venus) was formed and when it was joined to fire and water, iron (the alchemists' Mars) was formed. In this way, by a proper mixing of ingredients, all the other metals and minerals, even precious stones, were formed. A mixture of earth and silver, for example, produced lead (the alchemists' Saturn), and so on.

And now, many things will become clear to you if you place the four symbolic animals, each in its proper place: the lion in the North, Man in the South, the eagle in the East and the ox in the West.

And this also you must know: the philosopher's Sulphur is the quintessence of fire acting upon air; the philosopher's Mercury is the quintessence of air acting on water and the Salt is the quintessence of water acting on earth.

The Philosopher's Egg

1

Gentleness and Humility

'Two other men, both criminals, were also led out with him to be crucified. When they came to the place called The Skull, there they crucified him, along with the criminals – one on his right, the other on his left. Jesus said, "Father, forgive them, for they know not what they do." And they divided up his clothes by casting lots.
The people stood watching, and the leaders even sneered at him. They said, "He saved others; let him save himself if he is the Christ of God, the Chosen One."
The soldiers also came up and mocked him. They offered him wine vinegar and said, "If you are the King of the Jews, save yourself."
There was a written notice above him which read: THIS IS THE KING OF THE JEWS.
One of the criminals who hung there hurled insults at him: "Aren't you the Christ? Save yourself and us!"
But the other criminal rebuked him. "Don't you fear God," he said, "since you are under the same sentence? We are punished justly, for we are getting what our deeds deserve. But this man has done nothing wrong."
Then he said, "Jesus, remember me when you come into your kingdom."
Jesus answered him, "I tell you the truth, today you will be with me in paradise." '

Luke 23 : 32-44

As you well know, the subject of man has an important place in all my lectures and, this evening, we shall be talking about him again but from a point of view that is different from that we have taken in previous talks. What I am going to tell you is at the same time very clear and very complicated, because we shall be interpreting some very significant symbols.

Materialistic science holds that the whole of man can be reduced to his purely material components (cells, molecules and atoms); that he is nothing but his physical body. Spiritual science and all religions, on the other hand, teach that man has at least two non-physical components: a soul and a spirit. I do not intend, today, to talk about all the different systems elaborated by those who have thought about the different levels of man's being. Today we shall adopt the system implicit in Jesus' words: 'Love the Lord your God with all your heart and with all your soul and with all your mind and with all your strength'. We may conclude from these words that Jesus recognized the four levels in man: heart, mind or intellect, soul and spirit for, as we know from spiritual science, the only true power or force resides in the spirit.* We can also relate these four principles to the Hindu system, which is also the Theosophical system, and say that the heart represents the Astral body; the soul the Buddhic body; the intellect the Mental body, and the power the Atmic body. And these four principles dwell together in the one physical body.

It appears that many people cannot distinguish between the heart and the soul. It is really quite simple: both the heart and the soul are the vehicles of our emotions, feelings and desires but whereas the heart is the seat of the ordinary emotions which arise from the torments and sorrows, or the joys and pleasures of purely physical, sensual things, the soul is the seat of divine, spiritual emotions and impulses. The most

* See 'The Power of the Spirit', *Complete Works,* vol. 5

disinterested, purest form of love and the highest form of sacrifice belong to the Buddhic plane. It is only on this plane that man becomes capable of uniting himself with the most exalted beings of the universe. The relationship between the intellect and the spirit parallels that between the heart and the soul: the intellect or Mental body is the vehicle of the ordinary, purely human workings of the mind concerned with the satisfaction of man's lower interests and physical needs. The

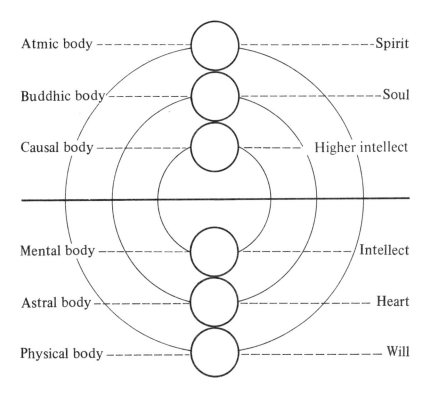

Figure 1

Causal body, on the other hand, is related to the Atmic body and is the seat of purely spiritual thought and mental activity.

The soul and the heart are two expressions of one and the same principle: the feminine principle whose field of activity lies between the lower level of the heart or astral plane, and the higher level of the soul or buddhic plane. Similarly, intellect and spirit are expressions of the one, masculine principle which manifests itself on the mental and causal levels. You see, now, how the two principles, masculine and feminine, manifest themselves in man through four different vehicles: the heart, the intellect, the soul and the spirit. These two principles and their four vehicles live together in one house: the physical body.

I know that many people have some difficulty in understanding this so I shall try to make it clearer for you with an image taken from everyday life and which corresponds in every detail. Imagine a house in which four people live: the master and the mistress, a man servant and a maid. From time to time the master of the house has to go away on a business trip and his wife stays behind, lonely and sad, waiting for her beloved husband to come home. And when he does get back, laden with gifts, it is an occasion for celebration. At other times master and mistress go away together for a long journey, leaving the servants alone, with nobody in charge of them. It is their opportunity to make the most of their newfound freedom and start exploring the storerooms and cupboards in which, naturally, they find all kinds of good things to eat and drink. And, as it is much more fun to make a party of it, they invite some friends to join them for the feast. Needless to say, after a night of orgy some of the furniture has been overturned and a few bottles – and perhaps a few heads too – have been broken. When their employers get home they are horrified with the sight that meets their eyes and they start meting out punishment and getting the house tidied up again, and before long everything gets back to normal.

Now, let's interpret this tale: The house, of course, is the physical body; the maid-servant is the heart and the man-servant is the intellect. The mistress of the house is the soul and the master is the spirit. Our spirit often goes away and leaves us and then our soul feels lonely and sad. But when the spirit returns he brings gifts: inspiration and an abundance of light and all is joyful again. At other times our souls and spirits go off together and then our hearts and minds hasten to do all kinds of foolish things together or with the help of other hearts and minds.

But we can learn a lot more from this story, particularly about the respective roles of the heart and the intellect, the soul and the spirit. In the first place, a maid's first duty is usually to serve her mistress whereas a man serves the master. On the other hand, of course, the two servants can also act together against the interests of their employers. The master and mistress of the house are separated from their servants by their whole way of life, their interests and activities, and they do not necessarily tell them the intimate details of their life and work or their plans for the future. Our souls and spirits act without revealing their intentions to our hearts and minds. But if a maid gains her mistress's trust by her irreproachable behaviour, her mistress may sometimes confide in her and tell her plans, her happiness in her love for her husband and so on, and the maid-servant – the heart – will be filled with joy because of what she has learned. Similarly, if a man-servant, the intellect, works faithfully and wins his master's confidence, he too will learn his secrets and thus gain in understanding and lucidity. But in order to arrive at this happy state of affairs, the two servants must live together in perfect harmony in the service of their employers. If they are always quarrelling and pulling in opposite directions they will only hinder their masters' work.

There are many more combinations and applications possible with this image and you should meditate on them, for whatever state of health or sickness, joy or sorrow, you may find yourself in, it can always be explained by the interaction of these four occupants of your house.

The bond which unites these four principles explains why the heart and the intellect, when they are not subject to the control of the soul and the spirit, never do anything right. The soul represents perfect love in Nature and the spirit represents divine wisdom in the spiritual world. Eventually, the two servants may become the son and daughter of God, but for the moment they are simply servants. A son must obey his father in everything, and a daughter, similarly, must do whatever her mother asks. So, when the heart and the intellect have learned to do God's will, that is, when they have learned to act with love and wisdom, then they will be children of God. As long as they continue to be disobedient and sceptical, full of suspicion and anxiety, they will continue to be the children not of God but only of man.

Now that you have this explanation in mind we can get back to the story of the two thieves who were crucified with Jesus. The Gospels give only the bare bones of what passed between them. The first thief taunted Jesus, saying, 'Aren't you the Christ? Why don't you save yourself and us, too?' But the other man rebuked him, saying, 'Have you no fear of God, since we are under the same sentence? We are being punished justly; we only get what we deserve. But this man has done nothing wrong'. Then he said to Jesus, 'Lord, remember me when you come into your Kingdom'. It is not by chance that the characters of these two thieves are so clearly depicted, for we find them everywhere, in all aspects of life and even within ourselves, for the scene of Jesus hanging on the cross between two thieves is also symbolic of man's inner life. You will soon see that the first brigand represents the intellect and the second the heart, and Christ, hanging there between them, represents the divine principle which manifests itself through the soul and the spirit in the form of love and wisdom, heat and light.

Now, let me tell you a little story: One day an old peasant was on his deathbed and he sent for the parish priest and the lawyer. When they arrived, the old man signed to them to sit by his bed, one on each side of him. The priest thought he had been sent for because the dying man wanted to confess his sins and the lawyer thought that he wanted to make his will. From time to time the old peasant looked at the two men with obvious satisfaction and then closed his eyes again without a word. A quarter of an hour went by like this, and then another and still the old man had not said a word. But the priest and the lawyer were beginning to lose patience and they asked the man's son to ask his father why he had sent for them. The son did so and his father replied, 'My son, I can die in peace now. All I wanted was to die like Christ, between the two robbers!' Of course, this is only a tale, but it is striking to realize that the lawyer symbolizes the intellect and the priest the heart and if they were dishonest (after all, it does sometimes happen), then they really symbolized the two thieves, in their esoteric significance.

As I was saying, the first robber represents the human intellect. And the intellect, which is full of pride, doubt, suspicion, scorn and criticism, always wants to see a miracle and, in spite of this desire and of the fact that miracles are taking place all round it all the time, it never sees them. The human intellect always thinks to itself: 'If God existed, He would let Himself be seen. He would give me wealth, good health, beauty and immortality. I would have the whole world at my feet. I would never suffer again.' According to the logic of the human intellect, God exists only for the purpose of looking after our affairs. As soon as this stupidly calculating mentality leads to some little mishap, it is God who gets all the blame; the intellect storms and rages at Him. As for the heart, as it is only interested in a life of joy and pleasure, it expects everything to go smoothly for it and when it comes up against bitter reality it is enraged to see that it is not loved and made much of wherever it goes.

If the intellect is not guided by the spirit it becomes a prey to pride; if the heart is not warmed by the soul it gives way to all manner of immoderate desires. At the slightest sign of opposition the intellect is filled with hatred and the heart with anger. He who is full of pride hates everybody because he realizes that they do not have the esteem for him that he thinks he deserves. He is preparing a very bleak future for himself because that constant anger that gnaws at him can only end by poisoning him. He becomes solitary and taciturn and lives apart, in frozen isolation. The heart, on the other hand, when it allows its passions to get the upper hand, is consumed by anger when it perceives that people or things it loves do not belong to it alone. Both the heart and the intellect descend into hell when they are deprived of the assistance of the soul and the spirit, that is of warmth and light, love and wisdom.

Mankind finds itself in this piteous condition today because there is no longer any communication between the lower levels of existence and the sublime regions of the soul and the spirit which alone possess the gifts of life and a new culture. Human hearts and minds are ravaged and tormented because they are isolated and ignorant. Only one thing can save them and that is to find their masters and to begin to serve faithfully. Then the heart will become a channel for the soul and torrents of love will pour through it; then the intellect will become a receptacle for wisdom, and the spirit will manifest itself in it. This is humanity's greatest need at the present time.

The first of the two thieves did not know that there was an absolute law of cause and effect. He was too proud to admit that he deserved his fate. The other thief, though, felt that he deserved his punishment, so he rebuked the first man: 'Shut up! You know very well that it is divine justice that is punishing us but that Christ is innocent.' From the astrological point of view, the first robber was born under the negative influence of Jupiter in bad aspect with Saturn. The second was born under the most negative aspect of Mars in bad aspect with Venus. The first had killed his own father and the second had killed his wife in a fit of jealousy.* The first had no regrets for

---

* The reader may be startled by these details which are not revealed in the Gospels but we must remember that the Master explained, at the beginning of this lecture, that he would interpret the scene of Christ's death between two thieves as a symbol of man's inner life. This statement: 'The first had killed his father and the second his wife', therefore, must be understood symbolically.

On the other hand the difference between the two crimes, one of the heart, which the criminal regrets and for which he is pardoned, and the other of the intellect, which the criminal does not regret, corresponds to clearly recognizable cultural phenomena or psychological types.

All forms of intellectual revolt are expressed culturally by a bitterly destructive critical attitude which ends by being a denial of the very existence of God. The libertinist and nihilistic movements and Nietzsche's philosophy, although slightly different from each other, can all be cited as examples of this. The rebellion against God which led the first thief to demand that Jesus prove his power is simply a reflection of his patricide. In murdering his father the son attempts to free himself from a tutelage which he feels as the oppressive hand of God, but his act cannot free him. This is the tragedy of the intellect manifesting itself in pride by asserting its personal power in an abortive act which only demonstrates its total lack of power: in attempting to dominate it only succeeds in destroying, thus voiding all possibility of domination.

The jealousy which drives a man to murder the wife he loves, on the other hand, is an unconscious gesture of reconciliation. The classic example of this tragic situation is that of Othello who confesses his crime and begs forgiveness for having murdered Desdemona. The gates of Heaven stand ajar for one who, in spite of his crime, still loves, even though his love be too violent and exclusive.

Psychoanalysis has shown that, in the subconscious of the male subject, the father-figure is the one we seek to deny (reaction of the intellect) and the mother-figure is the one we seek to possess (reaction of the heart), but that the two reactions can lead to the same crime. (Editor's note)

his crime, but the other one was sorry he had killed the wife whom he still loved.

The first thief refused to admit that he was guilty but the other one was well aware of his crime. He was humble and he knew that Jesus had not deserved to be crucified, and in this way he shared in Christ's sufferings. He was indignant with the first thief who mocked him, like the soldiers and the rabble who had gathered round. He confessed his crime to Jesus, saying: 'Master, I'm a criminal. I killed my wife, but I was mad with uncontrollable rage. I regret my act, but I know that you are the Son of God. Forgive me.' And Jesus answered, 'I know, I know. I tell you truly, today you will be with me in paradise.'

Why did Jesus answer the second thief like that? The question has already been discussed at length and some people imagine that he was touched by the man's attitude. Well, people who are unaware that the law of cause and effect exists can say whatever they please but it does not alter the fact that a great Master cannot be influenced by soft words any more than he can be vexed by criticism. He looks into the depths of a man's soul and sees all that he has lived through in the past, all that he has earned and all the debts he still has to pay. So, if Christ told the second thief that he would be with him in paradise that very day, it was because he knew that in previous incarnations he had earned it by his good deeds. In spite of his crime, therefore, the law of justice decreed that he should receive the reward for his good deeds. A man does not switch instantaneously from evil to good. He cannot do anything good if there is no element of good in him. If a few short seconds of repentance were sufficient to open the gates of the Kingdom of God, how is it that so many sinners who have recited their act of contrition are still in Hell? Jesus' reply demonstrates the power of true contrition, but even true contrition cannot atone for all one's evil acts. The good thief was allowed into paradise with Jesus, but only temporarily; later he would have to return to earth to continue to atone for his evil deeds. People who do not know the laws always give faulty explanations. A man who has never done anything but harm cannot enter into the Kingdom of God: no one can give him letters of introduction if he is not entitled to them, not even Christ for Christ is the first to respect the laws. True, all authority and all powers had been given to him, but he never used them to oppose the laws, only to set the example. He never uses his powers abusively or makes arbitrary decisions as human beings do when they have the occasion and the powers.

Most Christians imagine that Jesus acted without regard for the law and that he would cure every illness, but that is not so. He allowed many sick people to remain unhealed because it was their destiny to suffer still. He, himself, said, 'Other sheep I have which are not of this fold: them also I must bring, and they shall hear my voice; and there shall be one fold, and one shepherd.' And on another occasion he said, 'I have manifested thy name unto the men which thou gavest me out of the world... I pray for them: I pray not for the world, but for them which thou hast given me; for they are thine.' Why did Jesus not save the Pharisees and Saducees? Because he had not come for them, they were not counted amongst his sheep. This is the proof that the sheep who were destined to be saved by Christ were already counted, but Christians do not realize this. It is perfectly true that the philosophy, the doctrine he gave is for everyone... but that is another matter.

You will perhaps say, 'If Jesus was crucified it was because he had to pay for some faults.' No. Jesus was sinless; he was crucified for the salvation of men. As I said earlier, the crucified Christ hanging between the two thieves is a symbol of the inner reality of man in whom the divine principle is constantly crucified by the heart and the intellect. Our hearts and our intellects which should be taking part in the work of the divine principle, not only hinder that work but even treat it with scorn or deny its very existence. In this way Christ is perpetually being nailed to the cross within us between the two thieves: the intellect and the heart.

Pride and anger are two violent poisons and men do not know what antidote to use against them. Chemists know about antidotes to chemical poisons but on the psychic level they are unknown. Initiates are the only people who have ever concerned themselves with finding the remedies against pride and anger, and they are gentleness and humility. On the astrological level Saturn and Mars represent great Evil and petty Evil, whereas Jupiter and Venus represent great Fortune and little Fortune. And when Jesus said, 'Come unto me all ye that labour and are heavy laden, and I will give you rest... for I am meek and lowly in heart', he was extending a helping hand to all those who are in the grip of these two great tormentors: anger and pride. Meekness, or gentleness and humility are the two indispensable virtues of a disciple for they can resolve all his most difficult problems. A man who is gentle and humble is not weak, as people often mistakenly think. On the contrary, he is in possession of the warmth of a spiritual heart and the light of a spiritual intellect and his foot is set firmly on the path of power. All those who believe that if they cultivated the virtues of gentleness and humility they would have to be door-mats for everyone else to walk on are very much mistaken. He who is gentle and humble has accumulated great reserves of strength; he is always safe, for the Scriptures tell us that God puts down the proud and exalts the humble.

Those who are versed in astrology will understand best what I am saying; they know that the planets Saturn and Mars are considered to be negative factors of unhappiness and misfortune, Mars, when badly aspected, being the planet of violence and Saturn the planet of pride. So it is Martian violence and Saturnian pride which have to be counterbalanced and disarmed by gentleness and humility respectively.

A great many people cannot recognize pride and humility when they see them : they take one for the other. When you see someone who has a servile attitude in the presence of rich or powerful people, because he feels poor, ignorant and weak compared to them, you say that he is humble. And then, when you meet someone whose ambition is to establish the Kingdom of God on earth, you say he is proud. Not at all : you cannot tell if a man is humble from the way he grovels before the rich and powerful. Let him get some money and some power for himself and you will see if he is humble! Let him come up against some sore trial and you will see if he is humble before God! So many people rise up in revolt against God or even deny His existence when they meet with some minor problem in life. True humility does not involve bowing down before the rich and powerful of this world, but before God. True humility is to pray, to have deep respect for all things sacred and to safeguard what is sacred within oneself and around one. For some, obviously, Jesus was full of pride because he declared himself the Son of God, drove the merchants out of the Temple with a whip and called the Pharisees 'generations of vipers', 'children of the devil' and 'white sepulchres'. But in fact he was not proud; he was humble before the Lord, and faced with terrible suffering and torment he said, 'Father, not as I will, but as thou wilt'.

The proud man is the man who thinks he is the only one who counts, who imagines that he is independent of everyone and everything, like a light bulb which thinks it can light up the house and never realizes that if the powerhouse ceased to send it any electric current it would be in utter darkness. The proud man thinks that it is he who is the source of the phenomena which manifest themselves through him, whereas the humble man knows that he is not at the source of anything and that if he does not safeguard his link with heaven he will have neither strength, nor light nor wisdom. He never forgets that he is nothing more than a medium. Well, I do not want to insist on this point any more but I can tell you this : he who thinks that he is above every contingency and that he depends on himself alone, forgetting all about the source of all those forces which manifest themselves in him, will end, sooner or later, by losing everything he has.

Let me tell you a story: Once upon a time in Ancient Egypt there dwelt a man who spent his days breaking stones. He was very poor and very humble, and he worked by a road along which an Initiate travelled every morning. One day, the poor man asked the Initiate to do something to help him to escape from his extreme poverty and the Initiate, seeing that he was a good worker said : 'Go to such and such a place and there you will find treasure. It is yours. Take it and you will be rich.' So from one day to the next the poor labourer became very rich and he began to hobnob with all the most prominent citizens and gave wonderful parties. One day, the Initiate wanted to pay him a visit, but the labourer had forgotten all about him, so busy was he with all the grand people who were now his friends. So when his servant announced the Initiate, the labourer said, 'I'm talking to my friend the Prince at the moment. Let him wait until I'm free.' The Initiate waited for a long time and at last a servant came to tell him that his master could not see him ; he was too busy. As he was leaving, an angel who had come with the Initiate, said to him, 'Do you really think you were wise to help that man as you did? It is your fault if he has lost his soul and become so hardhearted and proud. It is up to you, now, to correct your mistake. In the future you'll know better whom you should help.' The Initiate did not have to be told a second time : he corrected his mistake at once and that is why the labourer lost his entire fortune and found himself back by the side of the road, breaking stones again. And the Initiate continued to go by, every morning...

If I were to ask you if you knew how to do the four basic mathematical operations, you would say, 'Of course! Everyone knows how to add, subtract, divide and multiply.' And yet, believe me when I tell you that these four operations are very difficult to do correctly. Have you never heard a mother complaining that her daughter has 'added up' with a good-for-nothing and that nothing will induce her to 'subtract' again? In human beings it is the heart that adds, and it is the only thing it knows how to do. It 'adds up' everything and gets everything all mixed up. It is the intellect that subtracts, the Soul multiplies and the Spirit divides. Just look at how this works out in a man's life: a child collects everything it can lay its hands on, good or bad. It touches, tastes and even eats all kinds of things, even things which may be harmful to it. Childhood is the age of the heart, the age of additions. When he gets a little older it is the turn of the intellect to reveal itself and the child begins to reject whatever is harmful, useless or unpleasant: he subtracts. Later again he launches into the process of multiplication and his life becomes filled with women, children, belongings of all kinds, extensions of his business, etc. And finally, when he is old he begins to think that he will soon have to leave this world for the next so he makes his will and distributes his belongings to others: he divides.

We begin by accumulating things. Later, we reject much of what we had accumulated. The good things have to be planted in order to multiply and increase. If we do not plant our good thoughts and feelings we do not really know anything about true multiplication. If we know how to plant, there will be multiplication and a rich yield so that then we shall be able to divide and distribute our riches to others. Life often confronts us with the four mathematical operations. Something nags at our heart which we ought to be able to subtract, and we cannot; or our intellect 'subtracts' when it should not, by rejecting a good friend on the grounds that he is neither very intelligent nor socially important. Sometimes we multiply weeds and neglect to plant beneficial plants. We would do well to study the four operations in our own lives. Later on we shall have to deal with exponential powers, square roots, logarithms and antilogarithms. But for the time being we must be content to study the first four operations because, so far, we have not even learned how to add and subtract. Sometimes we do an addition with a real gangster, at other times we discard a good idea or a high ideal simply because someone has remarked that with ideas like that we will end by starving to death.

When I was talking to you about the two thieves who were crucified on either side of Christ, I did not tell you that the reaction of the second thief illustrates a method which we can usefully put into practice in our everyday lives. I can just hear you thinking to yourselves: 'Let's hope it's something that will get quick results!' Everybody wants to find methods that will get sensational results in no time at all. The only trouble is that quick methods do not always produce the best results. There was once a student who went to study with a very learned professor. He was eager to learn everything, and as quickly as possible. His teacher told him, 'It is possible, but be careful: when Nature takes six months to produce something it turns out to be a pumpkin. An oak tree takes a hundred years. If what you want is to be a pumpkin, it won't take long.'

There are, of course, a great many different methods. Thanks to the Teaching I received from my Master I can give you some of them, very simple ones, which will help you to make progress. Today I want to explain a very easy exercice based on the words of the second thief. When you are in pain or sad and distressed, when you keep running into all kinds of obstacles and complications in your life, you should say: 'Lord, God, I deserve what is happening. I have not been obedient, nor kind, nor just. Please help me. I want to do better. Transform me, purify me.' If you do this you will feel yourself relaxing and expanding, beginning to glow, and when you feel this relief, this lightness, it means that you have come into the Kingdom of God, like the good thief to whom Jesus said: 'This day shalt thou be with me in paradise.' Unfortunately we usually fall back again into the same condition as the first thief and say the same kind of things he said: 'There's no justice in life. Everyone is happy except me. Why do I have to be the one who gets all the bad luck?' And then, naturally enough, darkness falls over us again. If, every day, you sincerely think that you deserve everything that happens to you because of your own weakness and ignorance, everything will change within you. You may think that this is not a very good method but I can assure you it is capable of transporting you into the Kingdom of God in no time.

I will tell you about an adventure I had years ago in Bulgaria: A friend of mine who lived in the little town of Doupnitza had invited me to stay with him. Every day, at lunchtime, we took a picnic out to the hills near the town and, one day, I was supposed to go out by myself and meet him there (he worked in an office and could not come with me). We had agreed on the spot where I should wait for him. On my way through the town I saw that people seemed to be upset about something, so I asked what had happened and was told that two murderers who were wanted by the police had gone through the town and hidden in the hills, just in the area where I had said I would meet my friend for our picnic. I thought I'd better go there anyway, because my friend would be expecting me. I had hardly started to climb the hill when I heard shouts behind me. Looking back I saw a crowd of people and amongst them some policemen who pointed their guns at me and ordered me to stop. I stopped, of course, and quickly put myself in touch with the invisible world with a silent prayer: 'Dear Lord, help me in this time of difficulty.' Their mistake was obvious: they took me for one of the fugitive assassins, and I learned later that it was because I was wearing a brown shirt similar to his. I stood and waited for all those people to catch up with me and when they got closer I could see that they were frightened: they really thought I was an assassin. I said to the policemen, 'You have your guns but I have something much more powerful.' They looked at me in astonishment without understanding what I was talking about, so I put my hand in my pocket and brought out my New Testament, saying: 'This is my weapon and it is far more powerful than yours.' After that they came up closer and asked me what I was doing there, so I told them I was waiting for my friend and that we were supposed to be having a picnic together. 'That's all in order', they said, 'but you must come with us.'

So back I went with them and I had a really impressive escort as I came back into the town. The news had been spread all around that one of the criminals had been caught. I walked along quietly because an inner voice told me: 'Don't worry, everything's going to be all right.' When I was taken into the police station I sat down and began to explain some passages from the Gospels to all those who were there. An hour later my friend was also arrested on the same hill where he had gone to meet me. When he gave my description the police realized that I had been telling the truth, so they explained what had happened and sent him down to the police station to fetch me. When my friend arrived he was astounded to see all the policemen standing round me and letting themselves be preached to! I was released, of course, and went outside where there was still a crowd of people waiting. When they saw I was free and learned that I was not the wanted man but the guest of my friend who lived there, in their own town, I was suddenly so popular that everyone wanted to talk to me, and, for the next few days I had many conversations with the citizens of Doupnitza. Later, when I was at the summer camp of the Brotherhood at Rila, several of them came and visited me there and we continued our discussions. And every year, after that, groups of people from Doupnitza would come up to see me in the camp by the lake.

I have told you this story at some length because that day, when I was mistaken for a criminal, thanks to my initiatic knowledge I was able to say, 'Perhaps I have to suffer because of some wrong I have done. Perhaps, without realizing it I have broken a law. But I want to do better, Lord. Please help me.' In every circumstance in life, even the worst, we must pray. When I murmured these words in my heart, I heard a secret voice within me saying, 'Don't worry. Today you will be in the Kingdom of God.' And it was true. It turned out to be a very auspicious day for me for I gained a great many friends and I have always had a very good relationship with the people of Doupnitza ever since.

If only we could accept whatever happened to us, day by day, with faith and inner docility and joy, it would change everything.

An immensely important undertaking is being planned in Heaven at this time and we are invited to participate in it: it is to introduce much more love and light into the world, to show men that humility and gentleness are capable of transforming them and making them happy. We must participate with all our heart and soul and with all our mind and all our energies in this magnificent task. Everywhere, throughout the universe, the most advanced beings of the visible and invisible worlds are preparing the coming of the Kingdom of God and His Justice. But the Kingdom of God has to come, first and foremost, in us: in our hearts and minds, in our souls and spirits where invisible powers are at work, infusing divine life into us.

And now, let us meditate quietly together for a few moments: 'For where two or three are gathered in my name, there am I in the midst of them.' 'Two or three...' This does not mean two or three people but the heart, the mind and the will. Each one of us is two or three in himself. You may be alone, but if your intellect, your heart and your will are united to Christ, then He is there, with you.*

This evening, those of you who want to ask for all that is most beautiful and heavenly will receive what you ask for, for the invisible world is here, with us, and your prayer will be heard. The invisible world is always with us and always hears us, of course, but sometimes it is more difficult to make oneself heard. This evening, because of the atmosphere that we have managed to create, the invisible world is very close to us.

And now I wish you peace, joy and light. May gentleness and humility heal the wounds that the two 'thieves', pride and anger, have inflicted on you.

Paris, April 2, 1938

* See lecture entitled 'Spiritual Galvanoplasty', p. 11, Collection Izvor No. 214.

2

'Except Ye Die
Ye Shall Not Live'

'And there were certain Greeks among them that came up to worship at the feast: The same came therefore to Philip, which was of Bethsaida of Galilee, and desired him, saying, Sir, we would see Jesus. Philip cometh and telleth Andrew: and again Andrew and Philip tell Jesus. And Jesus answered them, saying, The hour is come, that the Son of man should be glorified. Verily, verily, I say unto you, Except a corn of wheat fall into the ground and die, it abideth alone: but if it die, it bringeth forth much fruit. He that loveth his life shall lose it; and he that hateth his life in this world shall keep it unto life eternal.'

John 12 : 20-25

This passage from St. John's Gospel has much in common with another passage in which Jesus says to Nicodemus, 'Except a man be born again, he cannot see the kingdom of God', or with the passage in Genesis, in which God says to the first man, 'Of every tree of the garden thou mayest freely eat: But of the tree of knowledge of good and evil, thou shalt not eat of it: for in the day that thou eatest thereof thou shalt surely die'.

Perhaps the connection between these passages is not obvious to you at first sight, but if you will just have a little patience you will soon understand.

'Except a corn of wheat fall into the ground and die, it abideth alone: but if it die it bringeth forth much fruit. He that loveth his life shall lose it; and he that hateth his life in this world shall keep it unto life eternal'. If taken literally, these words are terrifying. We have to interpret them.

Although God had told the first man that if he ate of the Tree of the Knowledge of Good and Evil he would die, yet when Adam and Eve disobeyed and ate the fruit of the Tree, they did not die. The fact is that there is no such thing as 'death' in nature. What we call death is simply an altered state of mind or of matter. One who dies on the physical plane, for instance, is born on the astral plane, and when he has lived for a while on that plane he will 'move on' to the mental plane, and so on until he has completed the whole cycle and begins all over again, on the physical plane. All the Masters and all the great Initiates have taught this in the Mysteries: how to die in order to live.

We know that only a fraction of what Jesus taught his disciples was ever recorded, because St. John says that the earth would not be large enough to contain a full account of everything that Jesus said and did. What the Gospels give us are innumerable, identical fragments, like the bone fragments that enable Cuvier to reconstruct the skeletons of certain prehistoric animals. With the help of these fragments scattered throughout the Gospels, Initiates are able to reconstruct what Jesus had in mind.

Very few people have any idea that Jesus instructed his disciples in the essential disciplines: Alchemy, the Cabbalah, Astrology and Magic. They think the Apostles were ignorant, uncouth fishermen. As though Jesus would have chosen such crude instruments to be the vehicles of the highest, most sublime truth! Outwardly, it is true, the Apostles were simple fisher-folk without learning, but in reality they were very advanced beings who had already been Initiates and played an important role in the history of mankind as prophets and servants of God. Their souls and spirits therefore, were already prepared for the tremendous task they were destined to accomplish on earth. The Apocalypse contains many examples of St. John's vast knowledge of the Cabbalah and Astrology, and by their healing of the sick, the Apostles proved that they possessed very great spiritual powers.

Hermes Trismegistus said, 'That which is below is like to that which is above, and that which is above is like to that which is below.' This does not mean that that which is below is identical to that which is above. It is a question of analogy or correspondence, but if we know how to interpret all the relations and correspondences between objects and beings in the two worlds, this hidden science will unfold before our eyes and we shall understand all the most important questions in life. In the Garden of Eden, Adam and Eve were forbidden to eat the fruit of the Tree of Knowledge of Good and Evil, and the same applies to us. We have to refuse certain kinds of nourishment if we want to preserve our life.

How to die in order to live: this was the secret taught to adepts in the Temples of old. Death comes under the influence of Scorpio and, as you all know, a scorpion is quite an extraordinary animal: when it senses that its life is in danger, it inflicts death on itself. The disciple must learn to be like a scorpion and be ready to inflict the death wound – symbolically speaking – on himself. All genuine alchemists have Scorpio in the ascendant in their horoscopes. Scorpio is the sign which rules change and death as well as the sexual passions, and the generative organs are under its influence. Taurus, Scorpio's polar opposite in the Zodiac, influences the throat and mouth. You may, perhaps, have noticed that a woman whose neck is either especially thick or especially thin, may have difficulty in giving birth to children, or may even be unable to have a child, and a woman who over-indulges in sexual activity may have a hoarse, husky voice.

A similar interplay of influence exists between all astrological oppositions, and if we had time to study the signs in detail and see how they correspond to the different organs of the human body, we should certainly make some interesting discoveries.

Aries, which rules the head, is opposite Libra, which rules the kidneys.

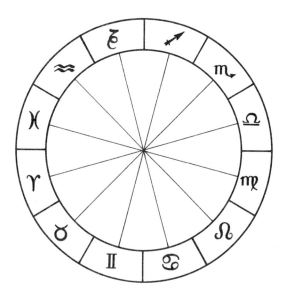

Gemini which rules the lungs and arms, is opposite Sagittarius, which rules the thighs.

Cancer, which rules the stomach, is opposite Capricorn, which rules the knees.

Leo, which rules the heart, is related to Aquarius, which rules the lower part of the legs.

Virgo, which rules the solar plexus and the intestines, is opposite Pisces, which rules the feet.*

But we must leave this subject for the moment. We shall come back to it at some other time.

Initiatic Science teaches that man is made up of several bodies. Above and beyond the physical body, he has an astral body, a lower mental body, a higher mental body (also known as the causal body), a buddhic body and an atmic body. This makes six bodies which are all closely interrelated in such a way that the human will corresponds to divine omnipotence, human feelings correspond to divine love and human thought corresponds to divine wisdom. Perhaps you will find all this a bit complicated: first I spoke about the three principles: heart, mind and will. Later I mentioned four: heart, intellect, soul and spirit. And now I am talking about six. Don't be surprised: those six may soon turn out to be eight or ten or even twelve! They are simply different ways of explaining how man is constructed and we may choose whichever system best suits our purpose.

Briefly then, and without wasting time on too many details, all these different divisions can be summed up as follows:

One is the Unique Principle, the Source of all being, the First Cause, the Supreme Being.

Two is the One made manifest, polarized as the twin forces: masculine and feminine, active and passive.

Three is the union of the two principles, masculine and feminine, to create a child. It is also the union of Love and Wisdom which gives birth to Truth.

Four is the four states of matter, the four elements: earth, water, air and fire, and the cardinal points of the compass.

Five is man, the five-pointed star, the pentagram, and the five virtues: love, wisdom, truth, justice and goodness.

* In this connection, see the two lectures in this volume, 'The Miracle of the Two Fish and the Five Loaves' and 'The Feet and the Solar Plexus'.

Six is the reflection of the Three in both worlds: it is the reflection of the world above in the mirror of the world below.

Seven is the Six united with one central point from which they draw nourishment and strength.

Eight is the repetition of the Four.

Nine is the three principles repeated in the three worlds: physical, spiritual and divine.

If you refer, now, to the diagram, it shows how someone who dies to inferior levels of action will be born in the world of divine action; how someone who dies to his lower feelings will be born to the higher sphere of feeling and how someone who dies to the lower levels of thought will be born to the higher levels of thought.

So this very simple diagram sums up the most extraordinary science in a nutshell and we shall often have occasion to refer to it in the future.

You will have noticed that two small circles are linked to the larger, concentric circles, on the level of each body. This represents something very important. In esoteric literature you will find this explained only in relation to the etheric body, which is the double of the physical body. The etheric double penetrates and envelops the physical body, giving it life, sensitivity and energy. If the bond between the physical body and its etheric double is broken, the physical body is simply a corpse: it dies. You know the story in St. John's Gospel of how Jesus brought Lazarus back to life: Lazarus' sisters, Mary and Martha, sent Jesus a message to tell him that Lazarus was ill. Three days after that, Jesus said to his disciples, 'Our friend Lazarus sleepeth; but I go, that I may wake him out of sleep'. But when Jesus reached Bethany he was told that Lazarus was already dead. Now, although it is perfectly true that Jesus raised Lazarus from the dead, yet he could not have done so if his etheric body had been separated from his physical body. Lazarus' etheric body was still united with his physical body, otherwise Jesus would have been unable to raise him from the dead, and this explains why he said, 'Lazarus sleepeth; but I go to awake him'.

It is the etheric double which makes it possible for the physical body to live and to feel, so that when the etheric body leaves the physical body in the course of a spiritualist séance, you can ill-treat the physical body and it will not feel anything. Doctors are beginning to study these things and one day they will discover that it is not the physical body that has sensation, but the etheric body.

So, just as the physical body has its double, the other bodies also have doubles: the astral body has a double which is of a subtler substance than itself, and if this double absents itself, the astral body will experience certain problems. The mental body, also, is permeated by a subtler double which gives it life and strength: if this double is not functioning properly, the mental body cannot think clearly. And the same holds true in the higher spheres: each body has its double.

And now, compare this with the way our own planet earth is constructed: Over the ground, the earth, there is water which covers a large portion of the earth and penetrates into every part of it. Over the water is the layer of atmosphere which is, itself, composed of two elements, air and fire (the sun's rays which permeate the air). This pattern of everything having its double can be found throughout creation.

Now look at this diagram (figure 2).

In the lower half of the diagram you can see that on the level of each body there are two small circles which represent earth and water: the lower circle, earth, is, as it were, the 'form' which must be permeated and vivified by water. In the upper half of the diagram, the form is no longer earth but air, which is suffused and vivified by fire. We have three bodies made up of a combination of earth and water, and three subtler bodies made up of the combination air/fire. The three higher bodies represent, as it were, the atmosphere above the

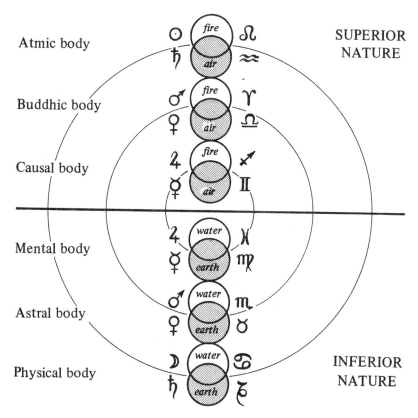

Figure 2

earth's surface. The twelve constellations of the Zodiac are represented in our six bodies, two for each body; and each planet exerts its influence in both worlds: the world above (the subtle bodies) and the world below (the denser bodies).

On the level of the physical body we find Capricorn ruled by Saturn and its etheric double: Cancer, which is its polar opposite in the Zodiac and which is ruled by the Moon.

On the level of the astral body we find Taurus, ruled by Venus, and its double (its polar opposite), Scorpio, ruled by Mars.

On the level of the mental body we have Virgo, ruled by Mercury and its double, Pisces, which is ruled by Jupiter.*

I leave you to find the correspondences in the upper half of the diagram, but I must just draw your attention to the fact that each planet has a favourable or higher aspect and an unfavourable or lower aspect and it is the lower aspect that prevails in the relations between the planets and the three lower bodies, and the higher aspect that influences the three subtle bodies. As the same planets are found on both levels they form a bond between the two bodies to which they correspond. This gives us the following pattern:

  ♄ ☽ the physical body is linked to the atmic body ♄ ☉

  ♀ ♂ the astral body is linked to the buddhic body ♀ ♂

  ☿ ♃ the mental body is linked to the causal body ☿ ♃

Mercury and Jupiter rule the two planes of thought (the mental and causal bodies); and Saturn and the Moon or the Sun rule the two planes of action and will (the atmic and physical bodies). We can see from this that the atmic body is under the influence of Aquarius, the thoughtful, creative man, and his double, Leo (the Sun), which represents the higher heart, whereas the physical body is under the influence of Capricorn and Cancer, that is of Saturn and the Moon. The sun, as we know, represents our individuality, or higher nature, whereas the moon represents our personality, or lower nature. We shall study this diagram in greater detail later on and see how it relates to many other questions. But, at the moment, I want to show you how it can help us to understand the Fall.

The earliest human beings lived on the buddhic plane, under the influence of Libra and Aries, ruled respectively by Venus and Mars. They lived a happy life in which joy, peace and freedom prevailed; they lived in union with God and all

---

* This formula intentionally utilizes only the seven planets known to traditional astronomy. (Editor's note)

the angels and higher beings. Venus, the ruler of Libra, gave them beauty and gentleness and Mars, the ruler of Aries, contributed energy and tireless activity. Thanks to the influence of Libra, the constellation of perfect equilibrium, all their energies were harmoniously accorded; they knew nothing of the tribulations caused by the two other constellations which are linked to these two planets: Taurus and Scorpio.

But Adam and Eve, who were accustomed to receiving the beneficial energies of Mars and Venus, gradually came closer to the two following constellations. Their eagerness to know led them nearer and nearer to Scorpio, which comes after Libra in the Zodiac, and Taurus, which follows Aries. And it was because they wanted to experience these unknown elements and energies that they committed the first sin: they moved out of the sphere of equilibrium and peace in which they had dwelt up to then and entered the turbulent regions of Taurus and Scorpio, the regions of sexual passions and violence. They died, therefore, to the life of Aries and Libra and were born to the life of Taurus and Scorpio and the forces of these two signs began to enter into them. They no longer lived on the buddhic level where all is joy and gladness, but on the astral level, where they had to experience suffering and convulsive unrest. We see, now, what God's warning to the first man meant: 'For in the day that thou eatest thereof thou shalt surely die'. Adam and Eve allowed themselves to be dragged down by the inferior energies of Mars and Venus and, in doing so, they died to the buddhic plane and descended to the astral plane. And this is what we call the 'Fall'.

In the past, when people wanted to study, they did not shut themselves up in a library and consult endless books. In the first place there were not nearly so many books as there are today, and people relied far more on their eyes and ears and on their memory. Teaching was mainly oral and based on the experience of life. Nowadays, most people learn from books and stuff their heads with all kinds of information which is not based on direct experience. You will find that almost everyone can discuss a host of different subjects with great erudition and quote from all kinds of famous authors, but very few experiment with things in their own lives. And yet, if you only knew it, the solution to every problem we meet with in life can be found already in the great Book of Nature. Nature has already answered every conceivable question: we only have to look in and around us. If you look for solutions in books you run the risk of finding so many different opinions that you will never be able to make up your mind which is the right one, whereas if you observe nature: insects, plants and animals and even the different physical functions in man, you will find the correct solution for yourself. A little while ago, we raised the question of that phrase: 'Except ye die ye shall not live', so now let us put the question to nature: 'How can this be?' and we shall see what answer we get.

Most people believe that to die means to disappear for good and, naturally, no one wants to die. Men cling to life and go to any lengths, even resorting to crime, to defend it. But the more they try to safeguard their life, the deeper they sink into death and pain. To die in order to live is, apparently, an absurdity, but in fact, it is the most important secret contained in the science of the spiritual life. Only those who want to die, who know how to die and who dare to die, are truly alive. Those who are ignorant, who go in fear and trembling of death are already dead. As I have said: death is simply the passage to a new level of consciousness, a change of region.

What answer does Nature give us? Where can we find creatures who die in order to live? Well, you have all seen butterflies, haven't you? But how many of you have ever stopped to think about the tremendous truth concealed by Nature in the life-cycle of a butterfly? What is Nature telling us by this metamorphosis of the caterpillar into a butterfly? The caterpillar, as we all know, is a loathsome little beast that can be seen dragging itself along the ground or on the leaves it devours. But it is also something of a philosopher: one day, thinking about itself and its life, it comes to the conclusion that it is really too ugly and ungainly and it decides to change. It retires into a cocoon and begins to look into the depths of its own being. Unknown forces gradually set to work to transform it and, when all is ready, the cocoon opens and instead of a caterpillar, there is a beautiful butterfly, robed in shimmering, diaphanous wings, flitting from flower to flower to enjoy the subtle delights of their nectar. As a caterpillar it was everyone's enemy, for it destroyed the plants and trees it fed on, but as a butterfly it is sought after and admired, and its food is all ready and waiting for it in the hearts of flowers. It is no longer obliged to steal in order to eat.

The transformation of a caterpillar into a butterfly is a symbol. A true disciple of Initiatic Science has only one idea in mind, only one desire, and that is to transform himself into a butterfly. (The caterpillar phase is something we all have to go through in the course of our evolution. For some it may last a very long time, whereas others advance much more rapidly, but no one can entirely avoid it.) At some point in his evolution, every human being is faced with the realization that he must die to his stifling caterpillar life, in which the splendours of creation are hidden from him, and be born to new life: the life of a butterfly, a life of joy, beauty and freedom. If a caterpillar refuses to stop eating leaves after forty days, it dies and in this case it is not a death which opens onto a new life; it is a final extinction.

Nature works with significant numbers and forty is the number of death, the number of Scorpio. The Hebrew letter Mem מ is the thirteenth letter of the alphabet. It corresponds to the letter M in our own alphabet and its caballistic number is Forty. This letter, therefore, is related to death and

its corresponding number, Forty, must be understood as a limit, but a limit which we must learn to overstep. We are told
that Jesus fasted for forty days in the desert and that Moses
spent forty years in the desert, where he, too, fasted for forty
days. If a caterpillar wants to remain as it is for more than
forty days it dies; but if it wraps itself in a cocoon and fasts, it
is metamorphosed into a butterfly. When it was a caterpillar
it destroyed the leaves by eating them, and everyone com-
plained about it, but now, as a butterfly, it is like a charming
young girl, attired more sumptuously than a princess and, far
from complaining, all the flowers are overjoyed to be visited
by such a ravishing, delicate creature. They stretch out their
leaves for it to rest on and offer it their corollas overflowing
with nectar to nourish it.

But a lot of human beings who are not so wise as caterpil-
lars, are only interested in eating the leaves of life. They refuse to admit that anything better and more subtle than that
exists. They declare, 'We have no intention of going to an esoteric school or of depriving ourselves of any of the pleasures
of this world. We intend to go on eating leaves: they are so
delicious!' People who think like that are making a big mistake for, in the spiritual life there are such subtle, delectable
joys that there is simply no comparison with the pleasure of
eating leaves. But a caterpillar cannot begin to imagine how
sweet these spiritual delights can be. To experience them one
has to accept to die to everything inferior. One must die to
hatred in order to be born to love, one must die to fear in
order to live in peace of mind, one must die to doubt in order
to blossom forth in faith. As soon as one dies to an inferior
level of sentiment one is born to a higher joy. God is not so
cruel and miserly as to want to deprive us of joy. On the contrary, He has prepared such marvels for our enjoyment that
they are beyond our imagining. As St. Paul said: 'Eye hath
not seen nor ear heard... the things that God has prepared for
them that love Him'. The spiritual life holds countless joys,

but we cannot acquire a taste for them unless we give up eating leaves, that is, our ordinary, earthly joys.

I am always astonished to find people who would rather eat gamey, tainted meat than pure fruit... but they exist! And it is exactly the same where thoughts and feelings are concerned: they enjoy thoughts and feelings that are tainted, like rotten meat. Once we have completed the span of forty days allotted to us by the Invisible World for the consumption of this coarser food, however, we are told, 'That's enough! It's time for you to retire into your cocoon now, and begin to work, pray, meditate and fast, otherwise you will have to die permanently'. At this point the true disciple understands and decides to change. Like the scorpion, he inflicts the death-wound on himself, dying to the world below in order to be born to a new, spiritual level of consciousness. This is the 'second birth' Jesus spoke of. If you refuse to believe the truth of what I am telling you today, I warn you that you will find it out to your cost at some future date.

And now, sit back and relax while I tell you a story of Nastradine Hodja*. First of all I must introduce you to Nastradine Hodja: as you know, most countries have their simple-minded folk-hero who gets into all kinds of scrapes. In Bulgaria he is called Hiter Peter and in Turkey he is called Nastradine Hodja.

Well, one day, Nastradine Hodja was up a tree, sawing off a branch, when a passerby saw him and called out, 'Hey! Nastradine Hodja: watch out. Can't you see you're sawing off the branch you're sitting on? You're going to come a cropper!' 'Mind your own business', said Nastradine Hodja; 'I know what I'm doing', and went on sawing. A few moments later, of course, the branch broke and Nastradine Hodja tumbled to the ground with it. As he picked himself up he thought, 'How did that man know I was going to fall? He must be a Prophet', and running after him, he called out, 'Sir

* Known in English as Mullah Nashrudin.

Prophet, since you were able to foresee that I was going to fall off the tree, you must know a lot of other things as well. Please, can you tell me when I shall die?' The other man was much amused by this and replied, jokingly, 'As far as I can tell from my astrological calculations you will die very soon... in three days, in fact'. Nastradine Hodja went home and told his wife, Fatima, that he was going to die in three days and asked her to get everything ready for his demise. Then he summoned his friends and told them: 'My dear friends, I'm going to leave you, but don't weep for me.' Fatima was sobbing and making so much noise with her lamentations that Nastradine Hodja decided to go to a quiet place in the forest and dig a grave in peace. So, taking with him all kinds of meat and wine he laid himself down in his grave and began to eat and drink, thinking that Mohammed the Prophet, in person, would come and fetch him (for he felt that he was to be counted among the just) and carry him off to Heaven where he would find mountains of delicious pilaff and quantities of beautiful girls waiting for him (he was much looking forward to this because Fatima was not at all beautiful!). So he was very happy and thought it was very agreeable to die. He had dug his grave right next to a hazel bush and from time to time a hazel nut would fall and Nastradine Hodja cracked it and ate it with enjoyment!

At last, on the third day Nastradine Hodja was aroused by the sound of footsteps and the tinkling of bells. Thinking that it was the Prophet Mohammed, with all his followers, who had come to fetch him, he sat up and stuck his head out of his grave to have a look. His sudden appearance startled the camels which reared up and started kicking, for instead of Mohammed and his heavenly retinue it was nothing more than a merchant caravan and they were so furious with him for causing all that uproar amongst their animals, that they jumped on him and thrashed him. Poor Nastradine Hodja dragged himself home, somewhat the worse for wear. 'Well,' asked Fatima; 'What's it like in Heaven?' 'Oh, it's wonderful', said our hero; 'You get a lot to eat and drink, but then you also get a thrashing. If you don't believe me, look!'

A lot of people behave like Nastradine Hodja: they prepare for death by laying up a store of meats and wines, in the mistaken belief that that is the way to get to Heaven!

The diagram I showed you (figure 2) will help you to understand the question of the caterpillar and the butterfly. The lower half represents the caterpillar which destroys the vegetation. According to its way of thinking the world was made for its use and enjoyment so, naturally, it has the right to lay waste to it without bothering about the laws of Nature... in fact, as far as it is concerned, the laws of Nature do not even exist. It lives out its narrow little life in obscurity and misery: narrow because of its destructiveness, miserable because its pleasures are purely physical and obscure because its thoughts are centred exclusively on itself. The upper half of the diagram represents the butterfly, free to fly through the air, to feed on nectar and to rejoice in the beauty of Nature. It represents the disciple of the divine science. To die to the enjoyment of leaves means to come alive to flowers and nectar. Freedom, joy, light and beauty: this is the world of the butterfly.

When I was living with a friend in Ternovo, in Bulgaria, many years ago, I worked very hard and read and meditated and experimented with various spiritual practices, late into the night. Sometimes I was so tired that I could not rouse myself for the sunrise in the morning. I was very unhappy about this because, like all our brothers and sisters in Bulgaria, we were in the habit of getting up for the sunrise every morning, in the spring. This state of affairs went on for quite a while and then, one day, a little bird got into the habit of coming to my window every morning, before dawn. It would tap on the

window-pane with its beak and wake me up. As soon as I
heard it I would call out, 'Hello! I'll get up at once'. The little
bird was so happy! It sang to me before flying away and, in a
few moments, it came back again with others to eat the
crumbs I put out on my window-sill. Every morning, before
the sun rose, that little bird came and woke me. Who sent
him, I wonder? I thanked him with all my heart because he
gave me so much joy. I felt that it was the Invisible World that
was awakening me through this little bird, and it gave me a
good example: I want to do as it did. At this moment I feel
like that little bird: I am tapping on your windows, saying:
'Wake up, the sun is rising, the sun of the new life, the sun of
Everlasting Love, Omniscient Wisdom and All-Powerful
Truth'. If you sleep through the sunrise you will be for ever in
darkness.

We must die to all our inferior, baser tendencies in order
to live in the realm of beauty, light and upsurging life. In this
way we may be a part of the new culture which is beginning to
make itself felt in the world, the culture of the new Golden
Age, the age of Love, Wisdom and Truth.

OM SAT TAT!

Paris, April 9, 1938

3

Living in Conscious Reciprocity
with Nature

There exists in Western tradition a mysterious and most secret science known as the Caballah, which sheds a great deal of light on these three words: God, Nature and man. From time immemorial man has been considered to be a miniature replica of the universe. In the ancient temples he was portrayed as the Key which opened the doors of the Palace of the King of the Cosmos, because everything that exists in the universe, be it matter or energy, can be found to a lesser degree in man. This is why the universe is known as the Macrocosmos (the great world) and man as the Microcosmos (the little world). And God is the name of that Sublime Spirit who created both the great and the little worlds and who breathes life into them and sustains them in existence.

In order to live and grow, this microcosmos (man) has, necessarily, to keep in touch, to maintain the bond with the macrocosmos (nature). He has to live a symbiotic relationship with nature: this is what we call Life. Life is nothing more than an uninterrupted, reciprocal give and take between man and nature. If this reciprocity is interrupted, sickness and death result. The food we eat and the air we breathe are the Life of God Himself. There is nothing in the whole universe that does not receive life and being from the divine Spirit. All things live, all things breathe, all things vibrate and are in communion with that torrent of life that flows from God into the whole of creation, from the greatest stars down to the tiniest atoms. St. Paul said: 'In Him we live and move and have our being'.

All is respiration, nutrition, continuous exchange. When the mind is engaged in thought it is effecting an exchange with the mental world; our feelings are the manifestation of an exchange with the astral world, and when we eat we are effecting an exchange with the physical world. This is why the three most important functions in life are those of nutrition, respiration and thought. If we stop eating we die; if we cease to breathe, we die, and if we stop thinking we die, too, although in this case, the dying is not physical.

Reciprocity, symbiosis, is the key to life. It explains all success or failure, all health or sickness, all beauty or lack of beauty, all wealth or poverty. Most people, although they are alive, yet eat and breathe in such a way as to clog up the channels of the body so that a normal exchange between themselves and nature becomes impossible and they fall ill. On the mental level it is exactly the same phenomenon: if you fail to nourish your minds with pure, luminous thoughts and if you neglect to clear out the baneful thoughts that clutter up your minds (just as you clear out dust and ashes from your house), then you will fall ill.

Often, when you complain that you do not feel well it is because you have not gone about this business of exchanges correctly: your hearts are not receptive; you are narrow-minded, bigoted and proud. You may think that it is intelligent to be like that, but what you do not realize is that this attitude erects a barrier between yourself and Nature: exchange is no longer possible. He who gives, on the other hand, he who is openhearted, is capable of reciprocity and a new intelligence awakens in him and he begins to understand even the most obscure problems. His friends may exclaim, 'Do you know that such and such a philosopher says exactly what you are saying?' No, he did not know and it does not matter one bit. What he does know is this question of reciprocity and exchange because he can feel it and he puts it into practice in his life. It is commendable, no doubt, to be able to quote philosophers and thinkers, but it is far better to be able to give living proof drawn from one's own experience. Instead of quoting all kinds of authors who are all more or less warped and vicious and who seek inspiration in bawdy conversations in rowdy, smoke-filled bars, it is far better to tune in to the only inexhaustible, immortal source: Nature. From now on we should quote only what we have learned from this great book which contains all wisdom. From now on let it be your only textbook. All men have to die and because of their lack of perfection, all men are subject to error, they make mistakes in what they write: only Nature is for ever alive and completely reliable.

A magus is simply a man who has a detailed and intimate understanding of mankind and of nature, and of the continuous ebb and flow that unites them through the medium of men's thoughts, feelings and acts. A genuine magus takes care to use only what is pure, noble and divine in his work, because he knows that every word or gesture as well as every thought or emotion, every act is magical. Whatever helps someone to progress along the path of perfection, whatever brings man closer to God, is white magic, whereas all that holds man back in his quest for perfection, whatever comes between him and the divine Source, is black magic. Whether it be conscious or unconscious, that is what it is. With this definition of magic you are now in a position to decide what kind of magic you perform: are you a black or a white magician? Like Mr. Jourdain, who had been speaking prose for forty years without knowing it, everybody performs magic all the time without knowing it. But if you point out to them that their black looks and vulgar gestures are black magic they get very indignant! The greatest magus of all is the sun: he only has to appear for everything in nature to burst forth into new life and beauty.

Many modern artists are purveyors of baneful influences. In fact most books, plays, films, paintings and musical compositions today are distorted creations which foul the atmosphere and degrade mankind. And if one ventures to point out that the public is being fed on inferior, poisonous fare, one is told that it is what it wants, because it is the only thing that has any flavour! For a show or a book to be successful it has to deal with spying, theft, adultery and murder, or else the blood sports: boxing, wrestling and bull fighting! No wonder then that these images remain active in the subconscious mind, night and day, until one fine day their unconscious hosts start manifesting their influence in some way or another. People forget that there is a sublime aspect to life which they should explore and present in their works, for it is the only way to improve and embellish our existence. It seems as though men are less and less able to find sustenance in that direction.

An Initiate knows the value, significance and depth of every sound, every colour, every form, every movement. He knows how they affect the human soul and he is able to discern and choose exactly the right word or gesture. He is fully aware and in conscious control of everything that flows from him so that it shall be harmonious and full of grace, beauty and sweetness. Then all creatures, even animals, are drawn to him as to a spring of clear water, or to a powerful source of radiant life. In the presence of a really great musician, if only for a few moments, you breathe in his musical atmosphere and, for a while, you, too, are a musician. In the presence of a true artist you become an artist and in the presence of a poet you begin to sense the poetry in things. But if you are in the presence of someone who is neither musician, nor painter nor poet, you can stay with him for a hundred years and you will never learn anything. That is why the Orientals say that in five minutes in the presence of a genuine Master you can learn more than in twenty years spent in the best university in the world. With a Master one learns the Science of Life because every true Master possesses true Life.

It is important to understand that true knowledge does not come from outside. Let us take a very simple example: You are the pupil of a very remarkable, very famous teacher and you are beginning to be quite learned yourself. Then, all of a sudden, you meet a pretty little 'teacher' (that is to say, a very pretty girl) and without more ado you forget all about your learned professor and become the 'pupil' of your unknown little teacher. Why? Because the illustrious professor produced wonders but it was all on the outside, nothing of any importance happened inside you, whereas with the pretty girl it is just the opposite: she teaches you nothing externally but her presence warms your heart and gives you wings! Sometimes we can listen to someone explaining a philosophical truth of great profundity and he does it marvellously, and yet we remain unmoved, whereas someone who uses much simpler language can move us to tears. An Initiate never gives his disciples very much externally, but he gives them a great deal within. Just as the Spirit works within us in ways we cannot comprehend, an Initiate lights the secret lamps within us and fills us with vibrant life. The world is full of people who can give us outward wealth or knowledge, but he who can give us inner, subtle treasures is a true Initiate.

Nature is the great book that we must learn to decipher. It is the cosmic powerhouse to which we must be connected. But how can we make the connection? It is very simple: the secret is love. If we love Nature we shall find a great force welling up in us. This is the force of love and it is a spring which, in its flowing, washes away all impurities. The waters flowing from the spring of love open up the clogged channels within us and release that marvellous exchange which brings us the elixir of everlasting life.

All men seek happiness. Whether they be learned or ignorant, rich or poor, strong or weak, all human beings pursue happiness. But happiness cannot be found in glory nor in beauty, it cannot be found in power or wealth or knowledge. Happiness can be found only in love. He who loves is above all contingencies. But I am talking about he who wants to love, not he who wants to be loved. He who wants to be loved shackles himself because he depends on the goodwill of others: if someone is kind to him today he will be happy, but if, tomorrow, he receives no sign of affection he will be miserable! Only the kind of love which expects nothing and which never changes is true love. Someone who loves like this is strong and free, he does not depend on exterior circumstances, he is in charge of his own destiny, above the reach of everyone and everything, beyond the reach of all evil. He who burns like a furnace heated to thousands of degrees transforms whatever touches him into light and if someone tries to harm him it only makes him shine the more brightly. But he who is lukewarm will always be vulnerable: if someone slights him or hurts his feelings he behaves as though it were the end of the world.

So we have to stoke the fires in our hearts until they reach millions of degrees then, whatever befalls us it will only increase our strength, warmth and radiance. When a stone falls onto the sun it only burns more brightly: this is the spiritual significance of pain and suffering. Difficulties and sufferings are strewn along our path in order to help us grow stronger and more luminous, so we should never just try to avoid them or get rid of them. We should make use of them to increase our inner light. We should not respond to difficulties either by trying to get round them or simply by a stoical stiffening of the will: we should try to understand and interpret their meaning for us: they are there for a purpose, to teach us something. If our only reaction is to resist they will keep coming back time and time again until we have understood.

Nature is the great book in which we must do all our studying. Gradually, as our attitude toward nature is modified, so is our destiny. If we believe that everything in nature is inanimate, we deprive ourselves of a certain degree of life, but if we believe that everything in nature is alive, then everything – the stones, plants, animals even the stars – will contribute to increasing the flow of life within us. And as the flow of life in our physical body intensifies and our spirit becomes stronger, true, perfect Life enters into us and circulates through the solar plexus, setting up a flow of harmonious energy. It is only then that we reach true comprehension. And true comprehension is in feeling.

One can always talk about love but someone who has never felt it, at least once in his life, is incapable of understanding it. Love, like wisdom, has to be experienced, known from within in order to be understood. Jacob Boehme, a well-known German mystic, was a cobbler. One day he had an experience which he had, no doubt, earned in a previous incarnation: he suddenly found himself and everything around him lit up by an intense, brilliant light, so brilliant that he found it unbearable. In a panic, he ran out of his house, thinking to take refuge in the country, but there, among the rocks and the trees, the grass and flowers, it was even worse. Everything had been transformed into light and he could hear the voices of nature speaking to him out of that light. Clairvoyants and mystics who have had this experience tell us that nature is transparent, lit from within, alive.

Warmed by love, souls blossom and objects open up like flowers as we approach. This is why, if we love nature, she will speak in us, because we are part of nature. Everything that exists in nature, exists also in us, although to a lesser degree, so that if we observe ourselves every day, we shall understand nature and draw her blessings on ourselves.

We are born of love (our mother) and wisdom (our father) and if we manage to resemble them we shall be truth. At the moment we are no more than the projected image of truth. St. Paul said, 'Now we see through a glass, darkly; but then face to face.' When this day comes we shall no longer look for truth in books, we shall receive it through a harmonious intercourse with the whole of nature. Most people are content to read: they fill their minds with all kinds of information which they then exhibit to others, but the lives they lead are in direct contradiction to what they profess to know. They attach no importance to the way in which they live or to the exchanges they could have with nature. And yet, if they only knew it, nothing can more effectively restore harmony within us, cure us of our illnesses and give us a sense of fulfilment than the way we live.

We must believe, and we must also learn to feel, that nature is alive and that we can relate to her through a bond of love, feeling that God manifests Himself through her. Nature is God's physical body.

In the Brotherhood, in Bulgaria, there was one brother who was particularly sensitive, and one day, in front of the Master and all the brothers and sisters, he told this story: He was sitting under a tree, one day, meditating, when he saw the tree trembling. For a moment he thought he must be hallucinating, but then, almost at once, he heard the tree saying, 'Please help me. There's a bit of wire in my trunk just below the surface and it hurts a lot'. The brother, rather naturally, was very surprised but he parted the tall grass around the trunk of the tree and, sure enough, there was a piece of wire embedded in the wood. He tried to get it out, but he needed a tool, so he said to the tree, 'Wait a moment. I'll go and get some tools, then I'll be able to set you free'. When he got back with the tools and got the wire out of the trunk he saw the tree thanking him by waving its branches. That is how alive nature is!

We are forever transgressing the laws of nature and we imagine that in spite of that, the Kingdom of God will be established on earth. But it is not possible. How can we expect the Kingdom of God to come while we still massacre millions upon millions of animals? The souls of the animals we have slaughtered and eaten manifest themselves in us in the form of instincts, passions, fear and cruelty, and we have a duty to educate them. That is why it is dangerous to eat animal flesh: their souls come and inhabit us and we have the responsibility of educating them. Who gave us the right to eat animals? Not nature, certainly! It is we ourselves. It would be different if animals allowed us to eat them, but if they do not allow it they have every right to live. To deprive them of their lives is a transgression of the law and it lays a heavy responsibility on us. 'Thou shalt not kill.' You are surprised by this, and perhaps wondering how you can possibly tell if an animal is ready to let you eat it. Well, it is very simple: go out to the chicken house, for instance, and try to catch a chicken and wring its neck. If it struggles and squawks as you pick it up, that is its way of saying: 'Master, I need to live a little longer. I haven't finished the work I came here for, yet', so you must not kill it. Don't deprive it of its God-given privilege of living a little longer. Let it go, and try to catch another one. If it squawks, too, let that one go again and keep on trying until you find one that does not protest, and that will be a sign that it is willing to sacrifice itself for you. And if you cannot find a single one that is willing to be sacrificed, what then? The answer is obvious: you must give up eating chicken and any other kind of meat. If you are fond of meat you will think that is a terrible conclusion. But that is because you never think of anyone but yourself! In all your reactions the only consideration seems to be your own pleasure and satisfaction, your own life. That is the only thing that counts in your eyes, even if it involves the death of innumerable animals.

Initiates know how costly it is to transgress the laws of life – one always loses more than one gains – so they prefer to give up meat all together. Do as they do and you will not be the loser. One is never the loser if one truly lives according to the laws of love. If you abstain from eating animals they will recognize you and love you and you will never again be tormented by their presence within you, like all those who kill and eat them. Those people are tormented by the souls of animals claiming compensation, saying, 'You have deprived us of the chance to evolve and learn anything more, so now you are going to have to take care of our education'. So it is not surprising that people who eat meat are surrounded by animal souls which they are obliged to nourish. Proof of this can be seen in the fact that meat-eaters show more cruelty, anger, sensuality and fear in their behaviour than vegetarians and that they often suffer from insomnia. All that is the result of that evil habit of eating meat. The law of Justice is relentless: mankind has been sentenced to pay for its crime of spilling so much blood in its slaughterhouses, by the spilling of the same amount of human blood. What butchery... and all for the sake of satisfying man's grossest instincts. How many millions of gallons of blood have been spilled on earth and cry to Heaven for vengeance! And are there no scientists to tell the world that all this blood evaporating from the earth attracts not only the microbes of disease but also thousands of millions of ghosts and beings from the lowest reaches of the invisible world, coming to glut themselves on these nauseous vapours? Is there no one clear-sighted enough to see the havoc all this blood is creating in both the visible and invisible worlds? Most human beings have sunk so low that nothing is really important to them except their own physical wellbeing. They like meat and they are going to go on eating it whatever the consequences may be.

But animals are not as stupid as most people think: they can sometimes see things far more clearly than men. In India, for instance, yogis meditate in the forests in perfect safety in spite of all the wild beasts: they know that none will ever touch them. How can one explain this? How can a snake or a wild animal tell the difference between a man who is pure and one who is not? If they attack those who are impure and leave those who are pure in peace, it must be because they can differentiate between them. But, how? A meat-eater, for example, has such a strong smell that a wild animal can immediately recognize him as an enemy who has devoured his brother-animals and so they revenge themselves on him. Whereas the odour of saints and vegetarians inspires respect in them and they don't touch them. Often, in India, when a wild animal is causing devastation in a village, the villagers call on a holy man from the forest, to come and get rid of it. For several days the holy man sits in prayer at the entrance of the village and the wild animals dare not attack: they will never transgress the law of sanctity.

Tradition tells us that, before the Fall, Adam's countenance shone like the sun and all the animals loved, respected and obeyed him. But after the Fall all the light had gone out of his countenance and the animals became his enemies. If animals no longer trust men, if birds take flight as soon as a man comes close to them and the whole of creation looks on man as an enemy, there must be some good reason: and the reason is that he has fallen from the spiritual heights which were once his home.

If men accepted, once again, to live according to the laws of love and wisdom, the whole world would be transformed and the Kingdom of God would appear on this earth. War is caused by the thoughts and feelings of men who have never learned to abide by the laws of love and wisdom. Those who pursue perfection would never desecrate the sacred temple of their body with the dead flesh of an animal – sausages, blood pudding, hot dogs and patés – which are neither aesthetic nor hygienic. Besides, we can read in the Book of Genesis that when God told man what he could eat, before the Fall, He said: 'Behold, I have given you every herb bearing seed... and every tree, in which is the fruit of a tree yielding seed; to you it shall be for meat'.

As far as fish are concerned, the situation is different, because for millions of years now, they have been in a situation in which it is very difficult to evolve. The Invisible World allows us to eat fish, therefore, because this helps them to evolve. Also, fish contain iodine, an element specially made for this age.

I told you that you should eat chicken only if the bird did not try to escape when you went to catch it and with fish the situation is similar: you could say that a fish that allows itself to be caught in a net is willing to be eaten; the others escape. I know you will find this a peculiar way of looking at things; you think that fish are incapable of thought and that they are caught because of their own stupidity. But what do you really know about the life of a fish and what it can or cannot do? We are only just beginning to find out about the extraordinary possibilities of dolphins. Perhaps fish have their own schools and teachers. And perhaps, as it is an extremely prolific species which faithfully follows the commandment 'Increase and multiply', their religious leaders think that a certain number of them should sacrifice themselves. It is fishes who first taught man the law of sacrifice which enables him to evolve. People who are born under the sign of Pisces are often excessively sensitive, possessed of a great deal of intuition and the desire to suffer for others, they are creatures of abnegation and renunciation. The Age of Pisces is the age in which Christ was born to manifest disinterested love and sacrifice.

What is important to understand is that all that exists in the universe also has its place in our own beings, although to a lesser degree. If we attain control of our own physical bodies, the mineral kingdom will obey us. If we can dominate our feelings, we shall be obeyed by water. If we control our thoughts we shall attain control of the air and the winds and if we can control and direct our inner fire, we shall be masters of physical fire.

What more can I say? This whole question of reciprocal exchanges is very vast. But there is one question that we could explore, and it is the question of how human beings exchange with each other. It is neither difficult nor complicated to effect an exchange with Nature. First thing in the morning, when we get up, we wash our hands and face and exchange something with water: the water gives us fresh force, our thought becomes clearer and we feel clean, light and lucid. Then we go out to see the sunrise where we receive waves of vivifying energy and exchange with the air by means of our breathing exercises, and so on. Throughout the day, that interaction with Nature is constant: we eat, drink, work, go for a walk in the woods, or in a garden, bathe in a river, stretch out in the sun... None of that is difficult.

It is quite another matter when it comes to exchanging with another human being: all sorts of difficulties and complications arise! Even the most learned have a hard time, so it is particularly in this area that Initiation can be of use in helping us to find the solutions. Look at a pair of lovers: one look at each other, and a raging furnace blazes in their hearts. They both burn with the same desire: to come closer, to speak to each other, to gaze into each other's eyes, to eliminate whatever keeps them apart. The forces boiling up in them soon catapult them into each other's arms. Why? Simply because of that urgent need to exchange. There is a great mystery here. How many tragedies (and comedies), how many lives ruined and fortunes lost all because of this need to exchange! And yet, in some cases, this need can have very beneficial results. All of you have had some experience in this area; in fact I imagine that you could teach me a thing or two! But I cannot see a single one amongst you who understands the mysteries of a true reciprocity, the kind of mutual exchange which can light up all your inner lamps, set the springs of eternal life flowing and confer divine omnipotence on you. But this question demands special examination which takes time: the manner of establishing this kind of reciprocity cannot be explained in a few minutes. Only those who are fully prepared can hope to achieve it. It is not simply a question of goodwill: one has to be fully aware of all the subtleties of it and very strong. Only an Initiate can fully realize what forces and energies, what invisible entities are involved when a man and woman effect an exchange. Only an Initiate can tell what will result from it on every level of their being, and whether it will be beneficial or harmful. But I can tell you one thing which will, perhaps, help those of my friends who find themselves in difficulty owing to their ignorance of the laws governing this question: our main strength lies in the beginning. If you open up the flood-gates from the very beginning you will never be able to stem the tide, if you let out all the wild beasts at once, you will never be able to capture them again. If you push a rock over the edge of a cliff you will be powerless to stop it; it will stop only when it reaches the bottom of the precipice. So, above all, take care of how you begin! If you do not let yourselves be guided by reason at the outset it is bound to end in disaster. The first exchange of glances, the very first handshake, the first time you come close to each other you must keep a close watch on yourself.

The essential science, that which is contained in the Caballah, is the science of God, Nature and man. God is the Father, the Supreme Spirit; Nature is the Mother who gives form to all things, and man is the fruit, the offspring of the Heavenly Father and Mother Nature. A fruit possesses the properties of its parents and man, therefore, possesses, in miniature, all the materials and elements present in Nature, as well as the power and the forces possessed by his Heavenly Father. So our happiness and our very existence depend on our will to keep this bond with our Heavenly Father and our Divine Mother intact.

In order to maintain this reciprocal union with our Mother, Nature, we must try to ensure that our food and drink, the air we breathe and even the light we see by are pure. The bond with our Heavenly Father is effected by means of harmonious gestures, noble sentiments, and lofty thoughts. The four elements, therefore, are our means of contact with Nature, and the three principles in man, will, intellect and heart, are our points of contact with the Spirit. When the disciple knows this he can tread the path of truth in all confidence; he feels himself to be physically and spiritually one with the whole of Creation. He becomes a Temple of God by his union with the four elements (earth, water, air and fire), and the Spirit manifests Himself through the channel of the three principles. Like his mother, Nature, he becomes a universal book, open to those who know how to read, just as the Initiates read the great book of living Nature.

Blessed are they who understand this brief summary of a science which has been verified and put to the test thousands of times by the true sons of humanity, the children of Light, for 'that which eye hath not seen nor ear heard' will be revealed to them.

Paris, April 24, 1938

4

The Unjust Steward

'And Jesus said unto his disciples, There was a certain rich man, which had a steward; and the same was accused unto him that he had wasted his goods.

And he called him, and said unto him, How is it that I hear this of thee? Give an account of thy stewardship; for thou mayest be no longer steward.

Then the steward said within himself, What shall I do? for my Lord taketh away from me the stewardship: I cannot dig; to beg I am ashamed.

I am resolved what to do, that, when I am put out of the stewardship, they may receive me into their houses.

So he called every one of his lord's debtors unto him, and said unto the first, How much owest thou unto my Lord?

And he said, An hundred measures of oil. And he said unto him, Take thy bill, and sit down quickly, and write fifty.

Then he said to another, And how much owest thou? And he said, An hundred measures of wheat. And he said unto him, Take thy bill and write fourscore.

And the lord commended the unjust steward, because he had done wisely: for the children of this world are in their generation wiser than the children of light.

And I say unto you, Make to yourselves friends of the
mammon of unrighteousness; that when ye fail, they may receive you into everlasting habitations.

He that is faithful in that which is least is faithful also in
much: and he that is unjust in the least is unjust also in
much.

If therefore ye have not been faithful in the unrighteous
mammon, who will commit to your trust the true riches?

And if ye have not been faithful in that which is another
man's, who shall give you that which is your own?

No servant can serve two masters: for either he will hate
the one, and love the other; or else he will hold to the one,
and despise the other. Ye cannot serve God and mammon.'

Luke 16: 1-13

It is very difficult to interpret this parable correctly and, so
far, I have never read or heard the true explanation, even
from a priest or theologian. The text is so full of what appear
to be contradictions that it seems quite incomprehensible.
And yet, in a little while, you will see that it contains some
very profound and very important truths.

Jesus points to the example of a steward who behaves un-
justly towards his master, and tells us we should imitate him:
'And I say unto you, Make yourselves friends of the mammon
of unrighteousness... for he that is faithful in that which is
least is faithful also in much'. And then, in apparent contradiction, he seems to praise faithfulness, for he adds, 'If therefore ye have not been faithful in the unrighteous mammon,
who will commit to your trust the true riches?' So Jesus en-
courages both faithfulness and unfaithfulness, and that is really peculiar.

If you want to get to the heart of this text and understand
it fully, you will have to be very patient. Before we actually
study the parable itself there are a few preliminaries that we
have to understand, because they throw light on the meaning.

In a previous lecture* I showed you an astrological diagram and we shall refer to it again, here, for if we know how to use it, it will enable us to interpret many obscure passages in the Gospels and other Sacred Scriptures, for it is not an artificial construction; it represents a reality which has been in existence for thousands of years. Look at this diagram again, carefully, so as to understand what I shall explain. As you can see a horizontal line divides the whole into two parts.

For thousands of years, men have tried to study their own nature and to understand the principle elements which go to make up the whole and they have elaborated different methods to explain man's manifold being. Some see man as twofold (good and evil, the higher and the lower, spirit and matter, masculine and feminine, positive and negative, heaven and earth). Others divide man into three (thought, feeling and will, which corresponds to the Christian description of man as body, soul and spirit). The alchemists divided man into four, in reference to the four elements. Astrologers divide him into twelve, in accordance with the twelve constellations. Hindus and Theosophists teach that man has seven bodies: physical, etheric, astral, mental, causal, buddhic and atmic. And the Caballists divide man into three or four, or again, into nine or ten parts. And, finally, for others, man is an indivisible whole. Whichever system one adopts it is always true; it just depends on one's point of view.

To make things simpler, let's say that man is a perfect whole, but that that whole is polarized, that is, that it manifests itself in two directions, it has two different aspects. Man is composed of two natures: a lower and a higher nature, and they both have the power to think, feel and act, but in opposite directions. The best way to realize this clearly is to observe oneself. Most human beings get everything mixed up: the thoughts and feelings of their lower nature and those of

* See 'Except Ye Die Ye Shall Not Live' page 35.

their higher nature are all the same to them; they see no difference. But for an Initiate the difference is obvious. To tell the truth, one cannot distinguish an absolutely clear-cut borderline between the two. They melt into each other like the colours of a spectrum (from afar the different colours can be clearly distinguished, but seen from close up it is impossible to tell exactly where one ends and the next begins). In day to day life, however, they can easily be distinguished.

The diagram I showed you consists of two halves which represent our lower and our higher natures and in each half there are three subdivisions, corresponding to man's three functions: intellect, heart and will or, if you prefer: thoughts, feelings and acts.

Man's different bodies, therefore, are:

on the lower level: the physical body,
the astral body,
the mental body,

on the higher level: the causal body,
the buddhic body,
the atmic body.

But it is possible to use other terms, and say that we have,

on the lower level: the physical body,
the heart,
the mind;

on the higher level: the higher intellect or reason,
the higher heart or soul,
the spirit.

You are perhaps wondering what the three larger, concentric circles in the diagram (Figure 3) signify. They demonstrate the connection between the higher and the lower bodies. The atmic body or spirit, which is divine energy, power and will, is reflected in the physical body which represents

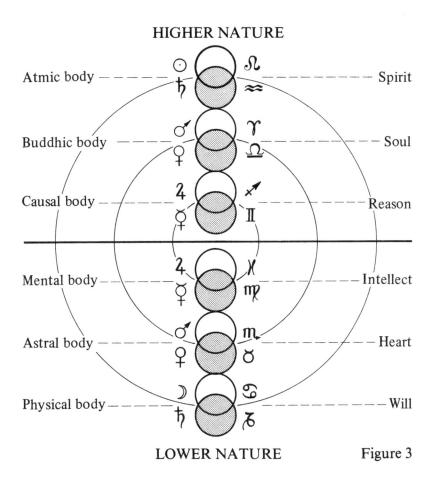

energy, will and power on the physical plane. The buddhic body or soul, in which dwell the highest feelings of love, self-sacrifice and kindness, is linked to the human heart or astral body. The causal body which is the vehicle of the loftiest and most luminous thoughts, is linked to the intellect or mental body.

All these correspondences can help to throw light on many of the darker moments of life as well as on obscure passages in the Scriptures. The most profound mysteries of the Divine world are concealed in the mineral kingdom and, more particularly, in crystals. This means that the alchemists who sought the most effective and powerful elements from which to prepare the Philosopher's Stone and the Elixir of Immortality, were right to look for them in the mineral kingdom. A crystal is a symbol of the absolute perfection that exists only in the Divine world. But we must leave these correspondences for the time being; we can come back to them again later.

I have already explained how the twelve signs of the Zodiac are divided into four groups, related to the four elements: earth, water, air and fire, with three signs for each of the elements. The following diagram (Figure 4) shows how they are grouped:

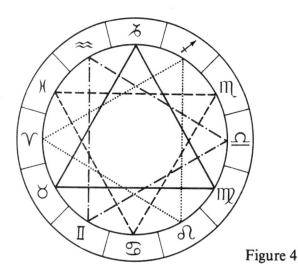

Figure 4

Fire: Aries ♈, Leo ♌, Sagittarius ♐

Air: Gemini ♊, Libra ♎, Aquarius ♒

Water: Cancer ♋, Scorpio ♏, Pisces ♓

Earth: Taurus ♉, Virgo ♍, Capricorn ♑

I shall not elaborate on this at the moment. It is sufficient to note that the physical body is under the influence of the Moon ☽ and Saturn ♄, and the atmic body is under the influence of the Sun ☉ and Saturn. The astral and buddhic bodies are influenced by Venus ♀ and Mars ♂, and the causal and mental bodies by Mercury ☿ and Jupiter ♃. The forms of the lower bodies are all in earth signs whereas their doubles are all in water signs; the forms of the higher bodies are in air signs and their doubles in fire signs. The lower half of the diagram, therefore, corresponds to the earth/water group, and the upper part corresponds to the air/fire group.

This is not an arbitrary arrangement, it can be found throughout creation. The planet earth is built according to this schema: first the ground or soil and above it the water which permeates the ground and completely covers part of it. Above the earth/water group is the air/fire group, that is fire, which is light, the sun's rays, permeating air just as water permeates the earth.

Astrology attaches a particular importance to the two Lights: the sun and the moon, for the earth is under their special influence. At certain periods it is the influence of the sun that takes precedence and at other times, that of the moon. The sun, the moon and the earth represent the threefold conception of man: spirit, soul and body.

The sun is the symbol of all that is stable, unchanging: our higher nature. The moon symbolizes the shifting, unstable aspects of man: his lower nature. Our passions, the purely human attitudes which make us cheat and steal from each other, all those worries and concerns that agitate us, our vanity and our thirst for praise, all our self-interest and egoism whose only concern is with our physical well-being; all this belongs to our lower nature. The higher nature, on the other hand, is formed of all our better tendencies: the desire to learn and become familiar with truth, to help others, to sacrifice ourselves, to be generous and loving.

A man who is dominated by his lower nature nourishes egocentric thoughts and feelings which are concerned only with the satisfaction of that lower nature. His higher nature is, as it were, hidden inside him and its manifestations are severely limited. But a man who is dedicated, full of respect for others and animated by the high ideal of becoming perfect in virtue, in such a man the lower nature diminishes in strength and the higher nature develops and becomes stronger.

To simplify things I shall call the higher nature 'individuality' and the lower nature 'personality' and, in a moment, I shall tell you why. In art (literature and painting, for instance), you will find many portrayals of the individuality and the personality. If you look at Daumier's drawings, for example, you will have an idea of the hideous aspect of certain personalities.

The personality wants, above all, to show itself off and is ready to go to any lengths, pleasant or unpleasant, to do so: it will wear eccentric clothes and gaudy colours, drawing attention to itself with loud, grotesque laughter and affected mannerisms. It is always trying to seem more important than it really is, like a hen that fluffs out its feathers and seems to be twice its real size. But, most important, it is extremely fickle and changes from one mood to another with incredible ease: in turn it will be gay then sad, optimistic and then discouraged, conciliatory and then vindictive. It is afraid of hunger, poverty and death and goes to incredible lengths to ensure that it will always have enough to eat and all the possessions it hankers after. But it is incapable of holding on to anything:

it is a bottomless pit into which everything vanishes. The personality knows only one motivation: self-interest, and to ensure this it is capable of changing its philosophy, its religion or its political convictions just as fast as circumstances require!

The individuality behaves in a way diametrically opposed to that of the personality. It is not anxious to show itself off, it never tries to bluff, it never draws attention to itself with loud talk; it knows that, when the time is ripe, it will be discovered. And until that day comes it relies on its talents and its own hard work. Rooted deep in the individuality is a steady, unshakeable conviction accompanied by staunch, durable faith and hope. It never wavers, its point of view is always the same.

The personality is represented by the lower half of the diagram, and the individuality by the upper half. The individuality makes itself felt through the most exalted virtues: wisdom (on the causal plane), love (on the buddhic plane) and truth (on the atmic plane). Each virtue has its corresponding power: wisdom gives man light, true knowledge based on the eternal, unchangeable principles; love brings with it life and happiness, and truth sets him free. Truth can give man happiness and life, but only if love serves as an intermediary. By itself, it is incapable of bestowing these gifts, on the contrary, in the beginning it often brings pain and torment. That is why so many people refuse to look at the truth: they are afraid of it. Wisdom, on the other hand, can free man and make him happy, also, but only if truth and love serve as intermediaries. Of itself, wisdom is powerless to free man or to make him happy, on the contrary it often has the opposite effect and makes him gloomy and pessimistic. As for love, it can neither liberate nor enlighten man: it can only bestow delight, joy and life. But love, wisdom and truth combined... Ah, there you have everything: the fulness of life, all of Heaven's blessings, the highest perfection.

Unfortunately, human beings rely on their personalities far too much; almost everybody looks for freedom, happiness and enlightenment from the lower side of their nature. They will always be disappointed: if one relies on the personality one will find only weakness on the physical level, suffering on the astral level and error on the mental level. In spite of its seductive ways, that is all the personality is capable of. Its moods are as ephemeral as a soap-bubble: it fascinates with its shimmering, fragile beauty, but it cannot last.

A moment ago I said I would explain why I use the terms 'personality' and 'individuality'. In ordinary speech there is no great difference between the two: people say that so-and-so has a strong personality or a strong individuality and the two terms can cover exactly the same reality. You will perhaps find other explanations in your dictionary, but when I use the terms to refer to the lower and the higher natures of man, I am referring to the Latin etymology of the word *persona*. The *persona* was the mask worn by an actor when he was on the stage. In the olden days, as you know, actors wore masks. Picture to yourself an actor: one day he has to play the part of a wise, reasonable man, the next day he may act the part of a criminal, a traitor, a seducer! Turn and turn about he is Cyrano de Bergerac, Simple Simon, Henry the Eighth or St. Louis of France. All these different parts represent the personality while the individuality is the man, the actor behind the mask, and he is always the same. This example highlights the fact that the personality is short-lived, just like a part which ceases to exist when the play is over; it only lasts one incarnation. In the next incarnation another personality comes on the scene, but the actor is still the same; the individuality remains itself although, of course, it develops and perfects itself in the course of the millenaries, thanks to the experience accumulated through the medium of its successive personalities.

All this is easy to understand: it explains how someone who is rich, healthy and good-looking in this incarnation, may, if he makes no effort on the spiritual level, return to earth in his next incarnation as a pauper, with neither good health nor good looks! On the other hand, someone who works to perfect his spirit and develop his divine intelligence or soul (while playing whatever part has been allotted to him in this incarnation), acquires qualities, virtues and spiritual treasures that will be his for ever, because they will become an integral part of his individuality. When he has finished acting the part of his personality he will be free to leave the earth, taking with him all his spiritual belongings, and travel throughout the universe. No one can ever deprive him of the spiritual wealth he has earned: it is truly his own. Just as a veteran of the stage who, thanks to all his different roles, has acquired a broader view of life and grown in stature as a man, every human being should leave this earth enriched by his experience.

And what of someone who has acquired only material wealth: what can he do when he leaves this life? When he has finished acting his part and it is time for him to go, he has to leave it all behind – that is the law – and he leaves this earth as a pauper, stripped of all his possessions. His individuality, with no spiritual acquisitions in its baggage, will be obliged to return to earth in the same way and be incarnated in the personality of a pauper: it will have earned nothing better. Someone like that is going to have to begin all over again and work very hard before he can get a job, some money and a house of his own, etc.

I am not saying that we have to do without all material belongings: clothes, private property and so on. No! All these things are indispensable as long as we are here, on earth, just as the stage-props and costumes are indispensable to the actor – but not more so. We have been sent into the world just as the steward in the parable had been sent to serve his master, and we do not have the right to leave that master, although he may dismiss us if we do not serve him well. When a man dies it is because he has been dismissed.

A peacock has very beautiful feathers and people love to admire them as he spreads out his tail and turns this way and that to show them off. He is obviously very much aware of those lovely feathers, and very proud of them. But if you go up to a peacock to get a better look at his tail, he will want to show off his voice too, and the shock of that horrible screech will soon make you change your opinion: you will no longer be so full of praise for peacocks! Well, the personality is exactly like a peacock. Someone who, instead of exerting himself to earn more wisdom, love and truth, is only interested in showing off, strutting about in front of his audience and bragging about how rich or intelligent or powerful he is – someone like that is a peacock who spreads out his tail and screeches, 'Look at me! There's no one like me in the whole world!' And then there is the nightingale: he never shows off. He does not have gorgeous, shimmering feathers, but what a voice! He is neither very big nor very handsome, but when he sings poets and lovers flock to listen to him. The nightingale manifests himself in a completely different way from the peacock, and he is a symbol of the individuality.

The personality and the individuality reveal themselves in so many different ways. Take a man who is always complaining that his evolution is being hampered by adverse conditions and who thinks that other people advance only because of all the advantages they have in life: this is the image of the personality. Take another one, in contrast, who never complains in spite of being in extremely difficult circumstances, and who devotes all his energies to developing his better qualities: this is the image of the individuality.

Or we could take an example from the vegetable kingdom: a palm tree, for instance. The date-palm grows in the desert: the sun scorches it, it has no proper soil, there is never enough water, and yet the palm-tree's reaction is to say, 'I'll show you what I can do in spite of the worst possible conditions', and the fruits it produces are sweeter than those of any other tree. The date-palm is a true alchemist: it transforms the desert sand into sugar! In contrast, one sees other trees growing in rich soil, well watered and with the advantages of a mild climate and they never manage to be any more than blackthorns, with hard, bitter little fruits. A lot of people are like blackthorns: they enjoy extremely favourable conditions but they bear only bitter fruits and they never stop grumbling. This only shows that they do not know what treasures they have within them nor how to put them to good use.

The personality is an inveterate grumbler: it is always complaining, insisting that if only it had a little more comfort and luxury everyone would be amazed at the marvels it would perform! But experience shows that there are a great many blackthorns and their like – symbolically speaking – which, in spite of the best possible conditions produce only insipid or bitter, sour fruit.

Now, let me tell you a story: There was once a very poor Bulgarian peasant whose one delight was to dance with his friends in the village square. One day there was a carnival in the village, and his friends were all there, leaping into the air and stamping their feet on the ground with great glee. But the poor peasant had no boots: he could only look on, feeling thoroughly miserable. At last, unable to bear it any longer, he asked a friend to lend him a pair of boots. When he had put them on and was leaping and stamping with the best of them, the owner of the boots called out: 'Hey! Don't stamp so hard. You'll wear out my boots!' The dancer was deeply humiliated, because then everyone knew he had no boots of his own. Then another friend said, 'Don't worry. I'll lend you some boots and you can dance as hard as you like', so the young man changed his boots and went back to join in the fun. He had hardly begun to dance again when the second friend called out, 'Go ahead! Stamp as hard as you like. If you wear out that pair I have another pair I can lend you.' The poor peasant went as red as a tomato with shame: for the second time everyone had heard that he had no boots of his own.

This is how the personality manifests itself in man: by calling attention to its good deeds. I know this was only an old pair of boots, but there are so many other occasions in life when a man's personality boasts of the good things it has done. Jesus said, 'Let not thy left hand know what thy right hand doeth'. In other words, the personality should not be told what the individuality does. Our good deeds should be done in secret because once the personality hears about them it will destroy them. This is why an Initiate is always very careful to hide the good he does. He knows very well that if he talks about it, other people will meddle and spoil everything.

And now I have another story for you: One day the Prophet Mohammed was taking a walk with one of his disciples. Suddenly, a man rushed up to them, shouting at the disciple, 'Ah! I've got you at last. Now I'll make you pay me the money you owe me!' To begin with, in spite of all the insults and the coarse language that was being thrown at him, the disciple remained calm and tried not to lose his temper. But after a while he could not contain himself any longer and before long the two of them were exchanging insults as hard as they could go. When they were both exhausted and the flow of invective had come to an end, the disciple looked round for his Master, but he had disappeared. After a moment he discovered him at the end of the street deep in meditation. 'Oh, my Master,' exclaimed the disciple; 'Why did you abandon me?' Mohammed replied, 'I never get between a snake and a tiger. It's too dangerous! When that man was insulting you and you kept quiet, there was a host of invisible entities all round you who were answering for you and protecting you. But as soon as you began to shout and defend yourself, these beings left you, and that is when I left you, too. There was nothing more we could do'.

When the individuality manifests itself it does not do so on the physical plane, in anger and violence, but through the medium of our higher nature, in wisdom, love and truth. At these moments we have power because we are allied with perfect beings who defend us, and our enemies eventually understand that it is they who are evil. This is why one has to be very patient and tenacious.

The personality cannot keep quiet for long: it makes all kinds of wild promises, weeps or laughs for joy and its mood is always changing. It is like the moon which is never the same from one day to the next. If you make the mistake of relying on someone who manifests himself through his personality, you will regret it when you find out how changeable and unreliable he is. The individuality, on the contrary, is a force we can rely on, as constant as the sun.

The personality is always pursuing its own, egotistical satisfaction. It does not worry about others (unless it is to its advantage to do so); it never asks if they are busy or if they are in trouble. It is interested only in getting what it wants. The individuality, on the other hand, is always interested in others, always altruistic. It is always concerned that what it thinks, what it wants, should be for the good of all. It is considerate and attentive, wise and prudent.

The entities of the divine world pick out those who are capable of noble, disinterested behaviour and bestow their gifts on them. And, as modern men confine themselves to living the life of the personality, they receive none of these heavenly gifts: happiness, liberty and life are withheld from them; they are inhibited, dependent and miserable. Just look at them: they are always complaining, they have no sense of direction, they feel hemmed-in and anxious, and all because they live only on the level of their personality.

How many human beings waste their whole lives in the attempt to satisfy their personality and that of others. A mother spends all her time trying to satisfy her child's whims, a husband tries to satisfy his wife's whims and a wife her husband's. And where does all that get them? Well, as the personality is ungrateful by nature, it immediately forgets all the kindnesses it has received and, instead of thanking its benefactors, it repays them with indifference, scorn or even hatred. If you try to please only people's personalities, their lower natures, you may be sure you will never be rewarded. In fact if you are repaid with misfortune, you have no right to complain, you will have brought it on yourself. Before you decide to sacrifice yourself for others, be sure to ask yourself what side of their nature you will be serving: the personality or the individuality.

The personality never remembers what others have done for it: it is ungrateful, weak-willed and treacherous. This is why, if you try to satisfy someone's appetites and whims or the demands of their sensuality, sooner or later you will be disillusioned. If you do not want others to let you down, you will have to exert yourself to cultivate their souls and spirits. In other words, you must endeavour to enlighten them and guide their steps toward the source, God Himself, so that, renewing the bond that unites them to Him, they may praise and glorify His name. A great many people are perpetually surprised when their faith in others is not borne out, but it is simply because they had been pandering to their lower nature. I have often heard parents giving their children advice calculated to ensure that they will always be able to satisfy their personality: they encourage them to cheat, they foster an insatiable appetite for money or pleasure, they teach them always to 'take care of Number One' without a thought of what it may cost others. Then, as the children grow up, they begin to apply this advice to the detriment of their own parrents who, of course, have completely forgotten that it was they who taught them to be like that!

Man's spirit is an unhappy prisoner, a king who has been dethroned by the personality which has taken over the reins of the government. He is locked up in a dungeon and fed on mouldy crusts of bread, given dirty water to drink and allowed only a glimpse of daylight through a tiny skylight. No one comes to his rescue, to set him free and restore him to his true place as sovereign lord.

Men attach importance to what you do to satisfy their appetites and their physical needs, but Initiates, the Angels and God Himself only appreciate what you do for someone's soul or spirit. What will be left of all the food you have given your friends if you never added a trace of that other food that lasts for ever. Ordinary men and women are incapable of nourishing or adding beauty or strength to another's spirit, but true Charity, the Charity of the Initiates, consists in restoring men's spirits to their rightful places, each in his own kingdom. Of course, it does sometimes happen that an Initiate has a care for someone's personality (he may heal someone, for instance, or help him financially), but it is always of secondary importance. Ordinary charity often fosters people's worst faults by encouraging them to be idle and take advantage of others while, at the same time, strengthening them in the conviction that to be charitable means to be naïve and gullible. Instead of helping people to become autonomous, self-reliant, useful citizens, capable of fending for themselves, charity sometimes turns them into social parasites.

Now that the difference between the individuality and the personality is quite clear to you, there is one more very important thing that should be stressed, and that is that the personality and the individuality must always go hand in hand. From what I have said about the personality you must not jump to the conclusion that we should utterly crush it or assassinate it! No. The personality must learn to serve the individuality. Without the personality, the individuality does not have the means to manifest itself. The personality is like the form, or the container, and the individuality like the contents. Form is necessary but it must express what it contains. If it is stupid and unresponsive, the human being is hamstrung and helpless.

Once the personality has become the servant of the human spirit, man will be capable of working wonders. You must realize that the only thing that prevents the spirit from understanding everything and from acting creatively in total freedom, is the personality. If you observe the people around you, you will see that those in whom the personality dominates are the most narrow-minded and prejudiced. But the slightest trace of prejudice in our philosophical or religious beliefs or in our attitude to other people or to our work, is always an obstacle to proper understanding and effective action. And nothing can be more prejudiced than an irritated, defensive personality, bent on revenge and ready to change its point of view at the drop of a hat. Since the personality's only motivation in whatever it undertakes is its own glorification, it is fated never to see the objective truth of reality. When an Initiate sees people with highly developed personalities coming to his school, he can foresee the problems they are going to have and the difficulties he will encounter in instructing them. The unequivocal axiom of an Initiate is this: the more one controls one's personality, in other words, the more one restrains and dominates oneself, the stronger and freer one becomes.

If I explained to you in detail what you are encouraging in your friends and relations, in the belief that you are helping them, you would be horrified. You think that you are nourishing them but, in reality, you are nourishing foreign entities living in them and of which you know nothing: strangers who eat and drink at your expense without so much as a thank you in return. The true science taught by Initiation is that which enables us to see exactly what entities we are encouraging and nourishing both in ourselves and in our friends.

Now I think you are ready to understand what the parable of the unjust steward means.

The personality and the individuality both have their allotted place in the great world, the macrocosmos or universe, as well as in the little world or microcosmos : man. In man, the seat of the personality is the abdomen or the lower abdomen, the area below the diaphragm ; whereas the seat of the individuality is in the lungs, heart and brain : the area above the diaphragm. The horizontal line, therefore, that separates the two halves of the diagram, represents the diaphragm.

Perhaps you are under the impression that everything that is below the diaphragm is without intelligence, feelings or movement, but this is not so. There is a brain, a heart and a will there, too. Now I have no intention of starting a new school of anatomy, but it is important that you realize that these two zones, above and below the diaphragm, represent two masters, and man has to learn to serve them both. When a man arrives on this earth he enters the service of a master : the physical body, that which is represented by the abdomen. But, sooner or later he is dismissed, that is, he dies. If he is wise he will reason as the unjust steward reasoned : 'What shall I do? for my lord taketh away from me the stewardship : I cannot dig ; to beg I am ashamed'. The intelligent steward knows very well that when he leaves his physical body, that eternally dissatisfied master, he will want to go on being active on the earth but he will not have the tools he needs. So, in order to satisfy the senses which continue to clamour for food and other pleasures, he will be tempted to 'beg', that is, to descend into the bodies of those who are still living on earth and to satisfy himself through them. This is what the steward who has been faithful to his personality is obliged to do : he becomes a beggar on the astral plane and continues to frequent the shoddy, disreputable places where the masses amuse themselves so as to join in the revelry.

But the unjust steward of the Gospels was intelligent : he had no intention of becoming a beggar-spirit. He used his reason and decided to win friends for himself through a judicious use of 'unjust' wealth : he reduced the debts owed to his master by his debtors. What does this mean? It means that, instead of continuing to give his stomach and other organs the copious meals and satisfactions most men give their bodies, he reduced the amount he would normally have felt he owed them. In other words, he put his personality on a diet by cutting down on his ration of tobacco, wine and women! Then he secretly diverted all the energy, time and attention he would otherwise have devoted to his insatiable master, to the service of his friends who dwell in the Tabernacles of the Just. In other words, he saved up some capital and deposited it in the heavenly banks so that when the day of reckoning came he would be recognized and welcomed. Instead of dedicating all his time and energy, all his affections, thoughts and feelings to his personality, he gave a proportion to his individuality. So he was 'unjust' toward his personality in taking some of its wealth and using it to make other friends.

This is the only interpretation of this parable that really explains why the steward was praised by his master. In the first place, who is this master who praised him? It is obviously not his personality, since it was his personality which had been cheated. So it must have been his individuality. His individuality tells him, 'You have been very wise. You were right to do what you did', for there is only one kind of injustice, only one kind of faithlessness which is allowed and that is an unjustice to the personality and all that is inferior and perishable. It is never permissible to cheat God, the angels, purity or goodness. And nowadays what do we see? Everyone is faithful to his stomach and his sexual urges, that is to his personality, and unjust toward God. Human beings are always ready and willing to satisfy their passions, their baser appetites, but they constantly cheat the Lord out of His due. I know quantities of men who are faithful to the barman at their favourite bar! Others are faithful to the 'tobacco habit' or some other vice or passion. Very few are faithful to habits of a higher order. But true fidelity consists in never neglecting prayer, study, meditation and fasting.

You will, perhaps, be wondering who the debtors were, whose debts were reduced by the steward, and also what those debts were. The debtors are invisible entities who are in the habit of taking certain spiritual elements from human beings and of paying for them with less subtle forms of energy and strength. The fact that the steward relieved those debtors of part of their debts, meant that he was willing to do without some of the energies he would have received from them, in other words he embarked on the path of abstinence (fasting, chastity, silence, prayer and meditation). These restrictive measures enabled him to do with less energy than his body was accustomed to receiving. When the physical body gives up some of its appetites, our higher nature is not required to supply so much energy and fluids, so it has a chance to grow stronger. But when our lower nature indulges itself too much our higher nature cannot manifest itself and is weakened, because it is our higher nature which supplies the energies needed to manifest on the physical plane.

As you will have noticed, Jesus does not say that the unjust steward relieved his master's debtors of the whole of their debt; only part of it. This means that human beings must not exaggerate the restrictions they impose on their personalities: they must not go to extremes of mortification and undiluted asceticism.

Jesus makes it clear that although man must work for the first master (the individuality), he is not entitled to leave the service of the second (the personality). He is not entitled to let himself be dispossessed of everything he has or to kill himself by deprivation. He must be 'unjust' toward his second master, but only up to a point. Take the example of a woman who is only interested in her physical appearance. She completely neglects her intellectual and spiritual development; all her time and attention are taken up with beauty treatments, massage and so on. And, of course, she gets results: she is extremely seductive, as sweet as honey, and she attracts flies and wasps from far and near! She has a great many friends and people like to invite her to their parties. All that is well and good, but after a few years she is no longer so attractive and her friends forsake her and she begins to miss them and to feel lonely and unhappy. People are only interested in inviting someone who has something to give, so now that she has lost her beauty she has no one to turn to for company and consolation. If that woman had imitated the unjust steward and been sufficiently intelligent to foresee that her master would end by dismissing her, she could have prepared for the change of situation. She could have begun to study and to develop her qualities of heart and mind so as to have friends against the day when she would no longer be beautiful. If she had been wise she would have kept her friends because she would have remained pleasing to look at in spite of old age. I have often noticed how women who cultivate their individuality become more and more radiant, glowing and charming as they grow older. Whereas those who have served their personality with exaggerated devotion become progressively uglier and more misshapen, because they live on a diet of regrets, envy, anger and hatred for everybody and everything, and their expression becomes more and more repulsive.

Since none of us can avoid the day when we shall be dismissed by our master, we should do well to prepare for it in advance and make friends in other, higher planes. For the friends mentioned in the parable do not belong to this level of existence; they are symbolic: 'And I say unto you, Make to yourselves friends of the mammon of unrighteousness'. Someone who is in the habit of eating a lot of meat: beef, pork, veal, chicken and sausages, builds up his physical body with all those cells stolen from the animals he has eaten. So he is going to have to make friends for himself by using the body he has built with unjust riches so that, when it is taken from him, he may be welcomed into the Tabernacles of the Just. How can he do this? By diminishing the dose! If you have always been under the impression that you owed your master (your stomach) five dozen oysters, a kilo of caviar, a dozen sausages, several turkeys and more besides, all washed down with the most expensive wines and followed by coffee, liqueurs and cigarettes, you can try to eat a little less! You will still be well fed and you will have released certain entities, who would have had to supply the energies you needed to digest such a meal, from part of their obligation to you. In this way you can win friends amongst these invisible entities and, when the time comes, they will welcome you into the Tabernacles of Eternity.

Restraint in the way we eat does not apply only to the physical level; it also applies to the joys and pleasures of the astral and mental planes which are also included in the personality, as you saw from the diagram I showed you.

Jesus also said, 'He that is faithful in that which is least is faithful also in much: and he that is unjust in the least is unjust also in much. If therefore ye have not been faithful in the unrighteous mammon, who will commit to your trust the true riches?' This means that if you have not been faithful to your individuality in small, earthly matters, you will not be considered worthy to be trusted with the great riches of the spirit.

This parable is proof that Jesus explained a great many things to his disciples but that the Evangelists reported only a small proportion of his explanations. Now it is we who have to interpret and it is not easy. There is one method of interpretation which consists of studying each word, of comparing the different versions and checking the translations against the Hebrew and Greek originals, of identifying the passages where something is missing or where there seems to be intentional or unintentional corruption or copyists' mistakes, of studying the historical context of certain questions, and so on. This is what is known as exegesis. Although everyone finds this kind of research fascinating, it must be admitted that it could never give us the key to an understanding of the Scriptures, even if we were to study it for the rest of eternity. I must confess that, although I have read a great many books on the subject, I am not really interested in knowing how the Sacred Scriptures were written or what mistakes have been made by generations of translators and copyists. It does not seem to me to be very important to know whether such and such a word has been well or badly translated. What does interest me is to find out what Jesus thought, what he meant when he spoke in parables, and it is very difficult to learn this through exegetical methods. But Jesus' words still live in the Akashic Record and it is there that we may discover their meaning if we are able to rise to that level. Once we have understood, on that level, we can come back onto the physical plane to interpret the text.

By the ordinary methods available to us, all we can discover is the literal sense, on the level of the form. But truth is not to be found on the physical level, confined to forms. We can discover truth only if we rise to much higher levels. The true meaning of the Scriptures, therefore, is on these higher levels and if we attempt to interpret them without rising to those levels we shall never fathom the true meaning. The first method: exegesis, is the method of the personality. The second is that of the individuality. The method used by the individuality allows the spirit to rise to those lofty regions in

which the meaning of all things lies hidden; the method used
by the personality, on the other hand, obliges the spirit to sink
to levels where only fragments and distorted vestiges of truth
are to be found. All the learned arguments and discussions of
the 'experts' only lead us farther and farther from the true
sense, the true content of the texts so that they become more
and more incomprehensible.

When our spirit rises to higher planes it encounters beings
who are more highly evolved and who know the great truths
contained in the Scriptures and can tell us about them.
Whereas the exegetical method leads the spirit to work on
lower levels where inferior beings can lead us astray. The
former method inclines men to humility by leading them to
compare themselves, unconsciously, with those superior beings encountered in the higher spheres: in comparison, they
see how ignorant, feeble and imperfect they themselves are
and humility begins to stir in their hearts. Whereas someone
who descends to lower levels, compares himself with ordinary
human beings, or with animals, insects or microbes, then, of
course, he acquires an exaggerated opinion of his own unique
talents and pride lays hold of him.

When a disciple looks up to and contemplates the advanced beings of the higher spheres he cannot help but recognize his own imperfection and see what a lot of work he still
has to do on himself. If he reacts with humility and an open
heart, then Heaven will shower blessings on him. But he who
compares himself with inferior, insignificant beings, shuts
himself up in his pride and arrests his own evolution. Pride is
an insuperable barrier. Jesus himself said so: 'Except ye... become as little children, ye shall not enter into the kingdom of
heaven'. To be a child does not mean that you have to be ignorant. A new culture is on its way: the culture of the child,
the age of simplicity, humility and love in which men will
compare themselves with Initiates, great Masters and the an-

gels, and will recognize the truth about themselves and realize how much they have to learn. Then wisdom, love and freedom will make their appearance in the world.

Most human beings learn through experience on the level of the personality. But this is wholly inadequate. Disciples and Initiates learn from the true Light, from the Spirit, and it is this that enables them to become clairvoyants, healers and prophets. Those who study in the schools of human personality also learn a great deal, but most of their learning cannot even help them improve their health, still less make them wiser or happier.

In the parable, Jesus mentions two masters, saying : 'No servant can serve two masters : for either he will hate the one, and love the other ; or else he will hold to the one and despise the other. Ye cannot serve God and mammon.' In other words we cannot serve both our higher and our lower natures. And a few lines farther on, the Gospel reports Jesus as saying, 'For that which is highly esteemed among men is abomination in the sight of God.' That which is glorious for the personality and for the world is odious to the spirit, the individuality. The personality looks for approval and applause from the general public, the ignorant masses, but the individuality seeks only the approval of the divine world.

This parable of the unjust steward is somewhat similar to a passage in the Gospel of St. Matthew : 'Lay not up for yourselves treasures upon earth, where moth and rust doth corrupt, and where thieves break through and steal : But lay up for yourselves treasures in heaven, where neither moth nor rust doth corrupt, and where thieves do not break through nor steal. For where your treasure is, there will your heart be also. The light of the body is the eye : if therefore thine eye be single, thy whole body shall be full of light. But if thine eye be evil, thy whole body shall be full of darkness. If therefore the light that is in thee be darkness, how great is that darkness!

No man can serve two masters: for either he will hate the one, and love the other; or else he will hold to the one, and despise the other. Ye cannot serve God and mammon.' We can see from this that Jesus must have spoken about this question of two masters on several occasions.

I have already told you this, and I repeat: you must not kill your personality. The personality is a tremendous asset when it has learned to be the docile servant of the individuality. Without our personalities we would be powerless to accomplish anything on this earth, but its role is to serve: if it tries to step out of the role of servant and play the part of the mistress of the house everything in man's inner economy is reversed and nothing makes sense any more.

So let us all do everything in our power to belong to the new culture of the spirit. Let us neglect our personalities a little, for they cannot be much use to us until they learn to submit to our individuality.

May the love which bestows true life, the wisdom which brings light and the truth which sets us free remain with you and in you.

Paris, April 30, 1938

5

Lay Up For Yourselves Treasures

'Lay not up for yourselves treasures upon earth, where moth and rust doth corrupt, and where thieves break through and steal: But lay up for yourselves treasures in heaven, where neither moth nor rust doth corrupt, and where thieves do not break through nor steal: For where your treasure is, there will your heart be also.

No man can serve two masters: for either he will hate the one, and love the other; or else he will hold to the one and despise the other. Ye cannot serve God and mammon.'

Matthew 6 : 19-21, 24

This passage from St. Matthew's Gospel should be read in parallel with Chapter 16 in St. Luke: the parable of the unjust steward which I talked to you about last week. In the first place, they both say the same thing about earthly treasures and they both conclude with the same warning about the impossibility of serving two masters: 'No man can serve two masters... Ye cannot serve God and mammon.'

I must emphasize, once again, that Jesus' words must be examined with extreme care, for everything he says has been carefully weighed, measured and calculated. 'Lay not up for yourselves treasures upon earth, where moth and rust doth corrupt, and where thieves break through and steal: But lay up for yourselves treasures in heaven.' From this we can see that Jesus knew that there were two, very different kinds of banks: the banks of earth and those of heaven, and both kinds of bank have numerous employees who are also very different from each other. But man himself represents both kinds of bank, functioning simultaneously in the same building: and both banks in man are branch-offices of the Cosmic banks from which they get their capital.

Don't be shocked if I use comparisons like this. Our visible world is built on the same pattern as the invisible world and its mechanisms reflect the realities of the higher spheres of life. That which is below is a reflection of that which is above; and I use the word 'reflection' deliberately, for the luminous beauty of the world above cannot be reproduced here, on earth. There are correspondences and parallels, however, which enable us to compare the two worlds and to understand the realities of the world above thanks to what we can observe here, on earth.

The two banks in man: the bank of heaven and the bank of earth, are the personality and the individuality that I explained in my last talk.

Generally speaking, the banks we know on earth offer their customers three different services: the first is that of a depository where they can keep their money in strongboxes and let their savings accumulate; the second service is concerned with loans and the exchange of capital. The third service is concerned with profit-taking and speculation. These three departments have their exact equivalents in the human personality: the strongrooms correspond to the physical reserves of the body; the department of loans and exchange to the astral level, the sphere of emotions and feelings, which is constantly involved in making exchanges based on interest. The speculative operations correspond to the mental level, the intellect, which is only interested in calculating how to make a profit out of other people's present or future insolvency.

So this gives us the following:

mental body – speculation
Personality: astral body – capital exchanges and loans
physical body – savings deposits, strongrooms

The banks we know in this world get rich at the expense of others. Pity is unknown to them although they always try to convince the public that all they do, think and feel is inspired by altruistic motives of love and respect for their fellow men! But the fact that men kill and eat sheep, cattle, chickens, rabbits and other animals; the fact that they domesticate horses, oxen, reindeer, camels and elephants for their own use, and that they slaughter other animals for their skins or their oil... surely all that is proof enough that man lives at the expense of others.

A few moments ago I said that every word Jesus spoke was full of meaning, so now I would like to show you the meaning of his advice: 'Lay not up for yourselves treasures upon earth, where moth and rust doth corrupt, and where thieves break through and steal'. First of all let's look at these three words: rust, moth and thieves.

Let's begin with rust: one always hears that alchemists tried to find the Philosopher's Stone because they wanted to transform base metals into gold. In fact many people think that that was the only thing that interested them. In point of fact, the Philosopher's Stone was the secret that would not only transform metals into gold, but that would also transform the fragile matter of which man is made, so that he would no longer be so vulnerable and so subject to temptation and disease. But we shall come back to that aspect another day.

Alchemy is generally thought of as the art of transmuting base metals into gold. Why gold? because gold is the only metal that does not tarnish and cannot be attacked by water, air or acids. It can only be dissolved in a solution of hydrochloric and nitric acid, known as *aqua regia.* Iron, on the contrary oxidizes very rapidly when it is exposed to humid air and the rust that forms on it gradually eats it away. Rust, therefore, can be seen as the symbol of whatever attacks metals or, more generally, the mineral kingdom. But the mineral kingdom is the lowest order in the hierarchy of natural kingdoms and symbolizes the physical plane in its entirety; rust, therefore, symbolizes whatever attacks and destroys physical reality including the human body.

Moths or worms, on the other hand, are more likely to be found at work in the vegetable kingdom and, in man, this corresponds to the astral plane, the level of the heart and the emotions. A man whose heart is devoured by hatred, scepticism, pride, contempt and violence is the victim of worms. And if one tries to get rid of a worm by cutting it in two the only result is that one then has two worms. This is very significant from the symbolic point of view and Greek mythology tells of the fabulous many-headed hydra of the marshes of Lerna whose heads grew again as fast as they were cut off. To kill it one had to cut off all seven heads at one blow. Hercules finally got the better of it by resorting to fire. The hydra represents the seven deadly sins which spring up again and again when we try to get rid of them. There is only one way of destroying them and that is to burn all seven of them at once in the fire of divine love. But all I wanted to make clear to you, today, was that when he spoke of moths or worms, Jesus was speaking of those enemies which attack man on the astral plane.

The thieves mentioned by Jesus are also a symbol. A thief comes to our house armed with skeleton keys and knife or gun, and after dark, when all the lights are out and we are fast asleep, he slips into the house. Thieves symbolize those who attack us on the mental plane. Someone whose intellect is in darkness or asleep will be attacked by thieves, for thieves love the dark. And who are these thieves? They are the invisible entities, the doubts and anxieties that dwell in you. Have you ever wondered why your thoughts so often leave you weak and exhausted, drained of all energy? Isn't this proof that thieves have ransacked your 'house' and stolen all you have? If you don't believe me, show me your treasures of strength, joy and peace. You have nothing to show? That is because everything has been stolen while you were asleep in the dark. Thieves have robbed you of your wealth. And the thieves are your own dark thoughts that rob you of all inspiration, all faith, etc.

The rust, worms and thieves that Jesus spoke of, therefore, correspond to the physical, astral and mental planes and we can indicate them on the diagram we used last week (Fig. 5).

One day a rusty old iron bar asked a ploughshare that had just come in from the fields why it was always so shiny. 'That's because I work hard', replied the ploughshare; 'But you do nothing all day long, you're lazy. That's why you're rusty.' If a man is lazy, his will will be attacked by rust; if a man is sensual, his heart will be devoured by worms, and if a man's reason is obscured, his mind will be visited by thieves. These are the three kinds of enemies Jesus warns us about when he says, 'Lay not up for yourselves treasures upon earth.' Look at what happens to someone who is only interested in the treasures of this earth: little by little he refuses to walk because he has a car, he never writes a letter because he has secretaries who do it for him, he ceases to speak since other people have been employed to speak for him, he ceases to think because others do all the thinking that is needed. The only things left for him are to eat, drink, sleep and keep his mistresses! By degrees he sinks deeper and

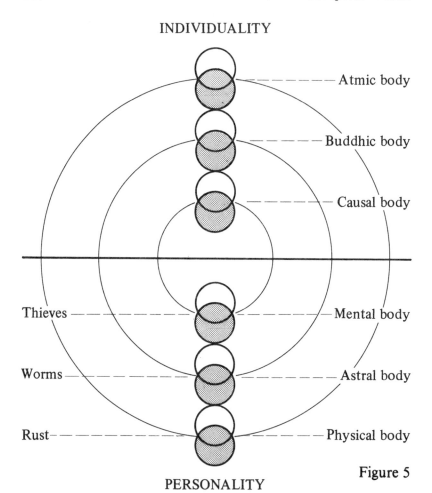

Figure 5

deeper into a state of inertia, where darkness and passions reign. The bank in which he has placed all his fortune will be attacked, sooner or later, by rust, worms and thieves.

Jesus himself explained the advice he had given his disciples :'For where your treasure is, there will your heart be also.' Yes, it is important that we realize this, for everything on this earth changes. We cannot keep our houses for ever, nor our factories, nor our cars; not even our wife, who probably has a lover (or our husband who may have a mistress!) nor our children who often grow up to be hostile to their parents. So, when the day comes when a man realizes he has lost everything that was dear to him, what is left? If your heart is in your strongbox, the day your strongbox is emptied of its treasures, your heart will be empty too. And if your love for your wife is purely physical, the day she leaves you your heart will be broken. So, when Jesus says, 'Lay not up for your-selves treasures upon earth... but lay up for yourselves trea-sures in heaven', it means: 'Break the bonds that bind you to the three inferior principles of your personality and ally your-self to the three higher principles of your individuality, and you need never fear the ravages of rust or worms or thieves again.'

It often happens that someone is deprived of worldly wealth because heaven wants him to learn something. If he is good and reasonable his poverty will spur him on to inner growth. In the first place he will learn to work hard in order to extricate himself from his poverty; secondly he will be com-passionate to others in a similar situation and will try to help them and, finally, being deprived of all kinds of exterior facili-ties, he will make the most of his opportunities to reflect and meditate. Poverty, therefore, is a very good school. God loves human beings and He knows that if He showers all kinds of material goods on them they will become lazy and interested only in their pleasures. Then thieves will break in and steal from them. So, to protect them from these dangers, He de-prives them just a little.

A few years ago in the United States there was an enter-prising gang of thieves who thought up a most ingenious strat-agem for the hold-up of a jeweler's shop, in broad daylight. They pretended to be filming a scene from a movie: as their car pulled up outside the shop, several men rushed out with guns in their hands and went into the shop while another man in the street pretended to be filming the scene. The thieves took everything they could lay their hands on and although the jeweller shouted for help nobody moved a finger to help him because everybody thought it was all part of the film. In fact they thought that he was giving a particularly good performance! It was only after the thieves had left and driven off in a hurry in their car that the poor jeweler also came running out of his shop and his desperate screams made the onlookers realize they had been watching a real live hold-up! But by then it was too late.

And you too can be robbed in broad daylight, for night and day are symbols. It can be darkest night in your minds, even at midday, and vice versa. 'Darkness' and 'obscurity' simply describe a state of mind in which we fail to see what the thieves are planning to do.

Why do you think there are more and more thieves nowadays? Simply because darkness reigns in men's intellects and the thieves who always work under cover of darkness make the most of the situation. But suppose, for instance, that more people were clairvoyant: then the plans that are taking shape in the minds of the thieves would be known, for thought creates waves and the waves would warn people that thieves were planning to come and steal their belongings. So, as they would be found out before they had even begun to steal, they would have to abandon their plans. No man-made law, no police force on earth, however well organized, will ever be strong enough to rid the world of robbers. They will continue to exercise their trade until men light all their inner lamps and open their spiritual eyes. Then the thieves themselves will sense that their day is over and they will be obliged to disappear or to reform.

Of course some people manage to laugh about thieves: one day Mark Twain was robbed and the following day he put up this note on his door: 'Notice to the next burglars: the silver has been replaced by tin cutlery. It is in the entrance hall, just on the right as you go in, next to the basket where the kittens sleep. You are requested to be very quiet as you steal this metal so as not to wake the cats because I am a light sleeper, too, and I have good ears. Rubber-soled shoes have been placed by the door: you are requested to use them, to put them back when you have finished and to close the door when you leave because of the draught.'

Now, let's look at the symbolism of a tree: roughly speaking a tree consists of two cones. The branches form the upper cone, with the point at the top and the roots form the lower cone, pointing downwards.

We have already discussed the symbolism of the two cones, so I shall not repeat that today. Let me simply remind you that the upper cone is the symbol of spiritual ascent and the lower cone the symbol of limitation. It represents Dante's inferno where there is neither light nor warmth nor any possi-

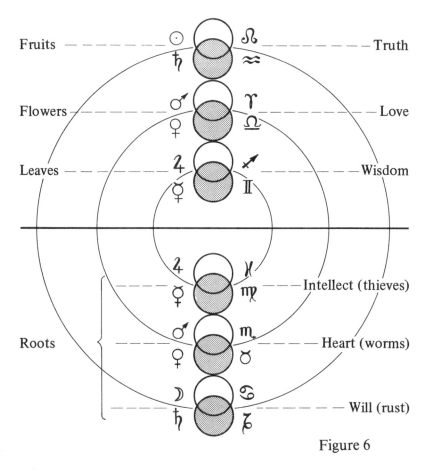

Figure 6

bility of movement. Someone who has sunk to the lowest levels of consciousness has cut himself off from light, warmth and movement. He is imprisoned in the roots of the tree which are the three inferior bodies: physical, astral and mental. Movement, warmth and light can only be manifested in the leaves, flowers and fruit of the tree. He who seeks to live in wisdom, love and truth, lives in the leaves, flowers and fruit: the higher bodies. The roots, therefore, prepare nourishment for the fruit which is ripening on the highest level of our being. And now, if you see where the astrological signs fit onto the diagram (Figure 6), you will realize that they correspond exactly: at the bottom, the Moon is linked to the inferior aspect of Saturn: laziness, for the Moon is unique in this. At the top of the diagram we have the Sun linked to Saturn's superior aspect: activity.

'Lay up for yourselves treasures in heaven, where neither moth nor rust doth corrupt, and where thieves do not break through and steal.' Now you can understand what Jesus was saying: the heaven in which we must lay up treasures is the heaven of love, wisdom and truth. For it is truth which prevents the corrosive action of rust, love that kills moths and worms and wisdom which protects us from thieves.

All these things that I have revealed to you can be read in nature, but our eyes have to be opened to see them. Someone who thinks he can get to Heaven without living a life of nobleness and justice and without any attempt to take the path of love and wisdom, is making a grave mistake and he will realize it later on, when he sees that the bank in which he has stored up all his treasures has become insolvent. One day, when he departs from this life, even if he was rich and highly esteemed amongst men, he will not be welcomed among the sons of God. He will be told. 'You've never made any deposits in this bank so there's nothing we can give you.' Perhaps he will reply, 'Don't you know that I was a celebrity on earth? I had a professorship in a well-known university. I was very learned... I had a great reputation as a scholar...' 'That's possible', he will be told; 'but things are very different here: here you are an illiterate. Show us what you have done all your life. You possess neither love nor wisdom. In other words you're an ignoramus!' And when someone is refused entry into the Academy of Initiates and Masters, he comes down to earth again and starts knocking on his friend's doors, shouting, 'Let me in. They've turned me out, upstairs!' and he starts sponging on others for his food. The world is full of souls who are still trying to satisfy their own appetites by feeding on others; on the pretext that the invisible world has refused to let them in they become vampires.

There is only one path to follow. Jesus said, 'Seek ye first the Kingdom of God and His Justice and all these things shall be added unto you'. Love, Wisdom and Truth: these are the Kingdom of God within us. The new culture which will soon be upon us is the culture of the Universal White Brotherhood. Thanks to that new culture we shall live in Divine Love which will give us the higher joy and happiness we long for, in Divine Wisdom which will illuminate us and in Truth, which will set us free.

Peace be with you!

Paris, May 7, 1938

6

The Miracle of the Loaves and Fishes

'After these things Jesus went over the sea of Galilee, which is the sea of Tiberias. And a great multitude followed him, because they saw his miracles which he did on them that were diseased. And Jesus went up into a mountain, and there he sat with his disciples. And the passover, a feast of the Jews, was nigh. When Jesus then lifted up his eyes, and saw a great company come unto him, he saith unto Philip, Whence shall we buy bread, that these may eat? And he said this to prove him : for he himself knew what he would do. Philip answered him, Two hundred pennyworth of bread is not sufficient for them, that every one of them may take a little. One of his disciples, Andrew, Simon Peter's brother, saith unto him, There is a lad here, which hath five barley loaves and two small fishes : but what are they among so many?

And Jesus said, Make the men sit down. Now there was much grass in the place. So the men sat down, in number about five thousand. And Jesus took the loaves; and when he had given thanks, he distributed to the disciples, and the disciples to them that were set down; and likewise of the fishes as much as they would. When they were filled, he said unto his disciples, Gather up the fragments that remain, that nothing may be lost. Therefore they gathered them together, and filled twelve baskets with the fragments of the five barley loaves, which remained over and above unto them that had eaten.

Then those men, when they had seen the miracle that Jesus did, said, This is of a truth that prophet that should come into the world. When Jesus therefore perceived that they would come and take him by force, to make him a king, he departed again into a mountain himself alone.'

John 6 : 1-15

In the passage we have just read, St. John describes how Jesus fed 5,000 people with two fishes and five loaves of bread. Many esoterics have discussed this miracle and they explain that Jesus invoked occult forces to multiply the loaves

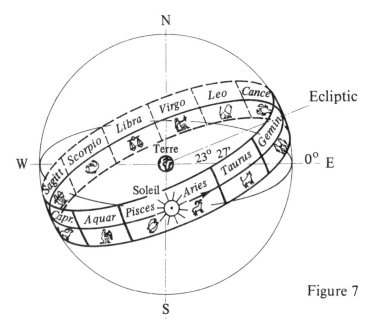

Figure 7

and fishes. But today I want to explain this passage to you from a totally different point of view and you will see, when I have done so, that it contains some of the essential truths of spiritual science.

But, to begin with, forget about the Gospel story and look at this diagram of the Zodiac (Figure 7).

As you know, the sun travels through the twelve signs of the Zodiac in the course of one year. The point of intersection of the ecliptic with the equator (0° Aries), which corresponds to the spring, or vernal equinox, travels through the Zodiac in the opposite direction to the sun. Every 2,160 years, this point leaves one constellation and enters another, and this passage is reflected by changes in every area of life. This new constellation brings with it new forces, new currents which begin to circulate and make themselves felt in the world. The Initiates of old knew what kind of influence would be exerted by the different constellations and this is how they were able to foresee events in the world that would be triggered by the change of sign.

All the major religions come under the influence of a complementary pair of signs in the zodiacal circle: Christianity, for instance is under the influence of Pisces and its polar opposite, Virgo.

The Gospels contain many references to these two symbols: the Fish (Pisces) and the Virgin (Virgo). The Virgin is a symbol that has existed from time immemorial. It represents Nature, inviolate, pure and chaste, who gives birth to the eternal Son of man, the higher Self or, as we say, the Christ. The symbolism of the Fish is also often used in the Gospels: when Jesus called his first disciples, Peter and Andrew, to follow him, he said: 'Come ye after me, and I will make you to become fishers of men', from which we see that men are compared to fish. Another day, when the Temple tax-collectors had told Peter he should pay the two-drachma tax, Jesus told him, 'Go to the lake and throw out your line. Take the first fish you catch; open its mouth and you will find a four-drachma coin. Take it and give it to them for my tax and yours.' There is also the episode of the miraculous catch of fish, which everyone knows, and then there is this passage

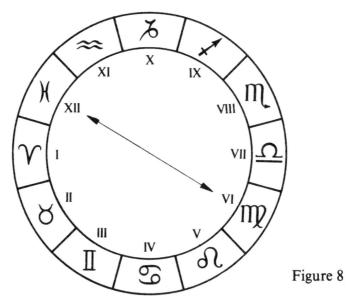

Figure 8

where Jesus says, 'Which of you, if his son asks for bread, will give him a stone? Or if he asks for a fish will give him a serpent?' It is not by chance that Jesus used these specific terms: fishes and bread are, in each instance, a reminder of Pisces and Virgo, for Virgo is portrayed as a young girl carrying a sheaf of wheat: the wheat from which bread will be made. And Jesus said, speaking of himself: 'I am the bread of life... I am the living bread which came down from heaven: if any man eat of this bread, he shall live for ever.' Fishes and bread: two essential symbols in the New Testament on which Jesus and his disciples must often have meditated.

And now let us see what astrology has to teach us about Pisces (fishes) and Virgo (virgin). From astrology we learn that Jupiter rules Pisces and Mercury rules Virgo. The Sages of old used only seven planets in their calculations (Sun, Moon, Mercury, Venus, Mars, Jupiter and Saturn), whose influence they shared out amongst the twelve signs of the Zodiac. But since the discovery of Uranus, Neptune and Pluto, modern astrologers teach that Pisces is also influenced by Neptune. This evening, however, we shall use only the seven traditional planets. We shall have occasion to use all ten planets when we come to examine other questions but, in any case, as there are still other planets to be discovered, the choice one makes is always somewhat relative.

As I have said, Mercury rules in Virgo and Jupiter in Pisces. Mercury represents an adolescent, whereas Jupiter represents a man in his prime. The two planets, therefore, are in sharp contrast in respect to size, activity, mentality and so on. Each of the seven planets is specifically related to a period in man's life: the Moon influences conception, gestation and birth; Mercury influences childhood; Venus influences puberty and adolescence; the Sun influences early adulthood, when young men are beginning to settle into a steady job and think of founding a family; Mars influences the full-fledged adult who has to struggle to keep his home and family together, and Jupiter rules the years of maturity: he is the *pater familias* who provides for his large family and whose position attracts admiration and respect from others. Saturn is the ruler of old age: he is the grandfather, with many children and grandchildren, and he is already preparing for his departure for the next world.

As we have seen, Mercury rules in Virgo. The symbol of the Virgin and child (Mercury) is a symbol of purity (Isis and Horus or the Virgin Mary and Jesus are examples of this symbolism). Jupiter, on the other hand, rules in Pisces, the sign of community life and self-sacrifice. These are the polar opposites, Virgo and Pisces (the Virgin and the fish), in which Christ manifested himself, and under their influence the Christian era has sought to develop the corresponding virtues of purity and brotherly love in the souls of men. Christ, born of the Virgin, manifested the virtues attributed to Pisces. Also you propably know that the early Christians used the symbol of the fish, not the cross: Jesus was referred to as Ichthus (Greek for 'fish'), a word composed of the initial letters of the words: *Iêsous Christos Theou hyios sôtêr*, meaning 'Jesus Christ, son of God, Saviour'. Each year, at midnight on December 25, the constellation of Virgo appears on the horizon and directly opposite it can be seen Pisces. Taurus is visible in the Zenith and opposite it is Scorpio (Figure 9).

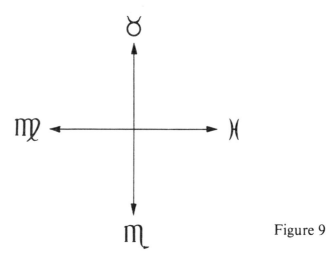

Figure 9

I shall not talk to you about fish in general: if you want to know more about them there are a great many books you can refer to. But I want to tell you about one particular kind of fish which is thought to be very intelligent: the eel. For a very long time the riddle of how eels reproduced puzzled biologists. In the first place, male and female eels do not frequent the same waters: the males stay close to the seacoast, in the mouths of rivers and saltwater lakes, whereas the females swim upstream into rivers and tributaries, lakes and ponds. And female eels caught in fresh waters contain neither spawn nor soft roe. But when scientists began to make soundings in the oceans, they found that every year, in autumn, all the eels of Europe, male and female, swim down to the sea where they gather together for the long, arduous journey across the ocean to the Sargasso Sea (between Bermuda and the Bahamas) and it is there that they reproduce. The larvae which then hatch from the eggs are carried across the ocean, back to Europe, by the ocean currents. The journey takes two years. By the time they reach the coasts of Europe, the young eels are seven or eight centimetres long; the males stay in the estuaries near the sea, while the females swim upstream into freshwater lakes and ponds. Specialists are still much intrigued by the question of why eels go all the way to the Sargasso Sea to spawn. This same area is the site of another natural phenomenon: it is here that a cloud front builds up, principally off-shore from Cape Hatteras, which then moves East across the Atlantic and the European continent.

The circle on the map indicates the spot, at 75° West and 30° North, at which these two phenomena take place: the spawning of the eels and the formation of the principal cloud-masses which cross our skies.

What is the influence at work at this spot? A true Initiate knows that everything in nature is interconnected: nothing happens by chance. Ordinary human science, which studies each phenomenon as though it were something separate and apart, often fails completely to penetrate the secret meaning of things, but for the divine science there are no secrets. That area indicated on the map is very important: it is the site of the vanished continent of Atlantis. In the past there was an

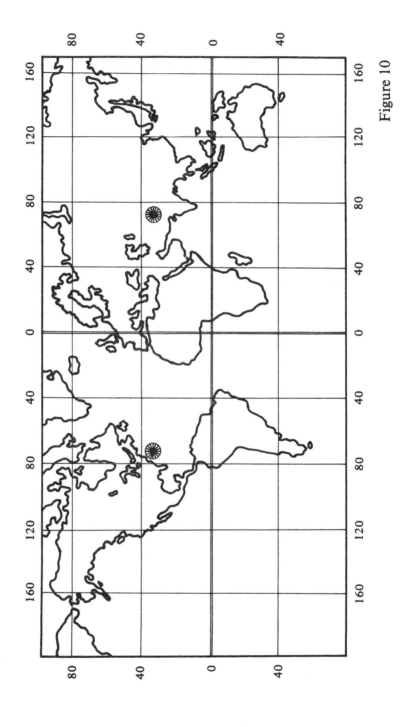

Figure 10

important Initiatic centre here, and its influence is still perceptible. But this is not the only reason for the eels' annual migration: there is another area on the earth's surface which is the source of the forces that manifest themselves in the Atlantic.

The annual migration of the eels coincides with the period when the sun is in Scorpio and Sagittarius. Scorpio, as you know, is the most mysterious of all the signs of the Zodiac. It is a water sign and it represents a serpent, a scorpion, an eagle and a dove. Some other day I will explain why the four animals which constitute the sphinx (ox, lion, man and eagle) correspond to the four zodiacal signs of Taurus, Leo, Aquarius and Scorpio. You will, no doubt, be wondering why the eagle is replaced by a scorpion. The reason is symbolical: the scorpion is represented instead of the eagle to symbolize the disaster that interrupted man's evolutionary progress. The eagle fell from the heavenly heights to earth, where it was changed into a scorpion: this is the symbolic representation of man's fall from his initial state of grace because of his lack of control and the misuse of his sexual energy. The same idea is symbolized by two other images, the dove and the serpent which, incidentally, were mentioned by Jesus: 'Be you therefore wise as serpents, and harmless as doves'.

The eels, which resemble serpents (and the etymological origin of the name means 'little Snake'), choose this particular period, when the sun is in Scorpio, to migrate. They take six months to reach their destination, getting there just when the sun enters Taurus.

Another, parallel, phenomenon occurs at the very same time, although on a totally different level: a mysterious command reaches all the human 'eels' of the world (that is: the Initiates who 'swim' in the cosmic ocean of life), calling on them to gather in a particular spot in the Himalayas located diametrically opposite the eels' spawning ground. When the moon is full in the month of May, the Initiates of the world are drawn, as by a magnet, to this one spot, just as the eels are drawn to the Sargasso Sea. And today, May 14, the moon is full and will enter Sagittarius at midnight. Tonight, therefore, the souls and spirits of the Initiates of the world will gather in the Himalayas, where they will take part in an important ceremony in the presence of the great Masters of humanity.

Just as the eels gather in the Sargasso Sea to produce their young, the Initiates gather in the Himalayas to give birth to the purest and most exalted thoughts and feelings to shower on mankind. If you look at the map again you will see this spot in the Himalayas indicated: as you can see it is exactly opposite the Sargasso Sea, at 75° East and 30° North. That is the Initiates meeting place.

As I said, this gathering takes place in May when the sun is still in Taurus, the most fertile and prolific sign of the Zodiac. At the same moment, the eels which left Europe with the sun in Scorpio (the polar opposite of Taurus), are spawning in the Sargasso Sea (diametrically opposite the Himalayas). The whole phenomenon is most extraordinary.

It is not normally allowed to reveal these things but, this evening, I received permission to tell you just a little about it, although what I have told you is not for everyone. Perhaps, later this evening, some of you will be able to accompany the Initiates to the Himalayas and witness the marvellous work they accomplish there.

We can now get back to the account of the multiplication of the loaves and fishes.

You already know that each part of our body is related in a special way to one of the signs of the Zodiac and, according to astrology, the solar plexus is related to Virgo and the feet to Pisces. And since Virgo and Pisces are interrelated and constitute the Christic polarity, there is also a special relationship between the feet and the solar plexus.*

* See the following lecture, 'The Feet and the Solar Plexus'.

The solar plexus is part of the sympathetic nerve-system which is a network of ganglia, nerve-fibres and branches, as you can see from this very schematic sketch :

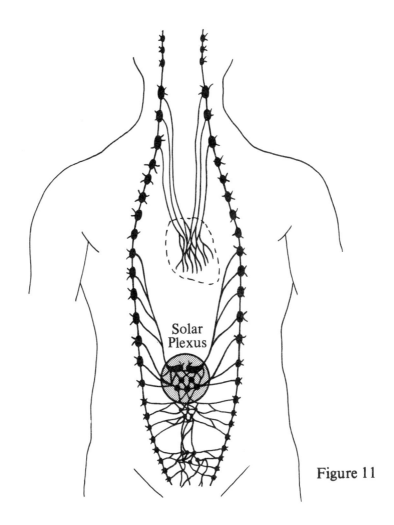

Figure 11

The ganglia of the sympathetic nerve-system

We shall come back to this question in greater detail another day, but for the time being let us study the solar plexus. It is located behind the stomach and consists of five ordinary ganglia and two so-called half-moon ganglia shaped like fishes. These are the five loaves and two fishes, united in the solar plexus. The male eel stays in coastal waters and river mouths, whereas the female eel swims upstream and stays in lakes and ponds until the sun enters the constellation of Scorpio: at that moment, males and females go, together, to the Sargasso Sea to spawn. This life of alternate separation and union is quite extraordinary. The two fish-shaped glands in the solar plexus represent the moon, which is why they are called 'half-moon'.

When Jesus was twelve he left Jerusalem, which is also at 30° North, and travelled to the Himalayas where he was instructed by Initiates in the great mysteries of nature and life. Some of you may be indignant at hearing this because the Gospels make no mention of any such journey to the Himalayas and besides, you may think, since Jesus was the Son of God, he knew everything. He did not need to be taught by others. Well, in that case, what do you think Jesus did between the ages of twelve and thirty? What is the meaning of this great gap of eighteen years in the Gospel accounts of his life?

For an Initiate the thing is quite clear: every human being born on this earth, even if he be a son of God, endowed with immense knowledge, still needs to learn. In order to free that hidden knowledge from its dense envelope of matter even the sons of God need to find themselves in conditions conducive to the awakening of all their powers and virtues. So Jesus had to be initiated. Someone who is ignorant of the necessary phases of human evolution may refuse to accept this explanation, arguing that Jesus was omniscient and all-powerful. But if that were so, how can they explain the passage in the Gospels which says that, after fasting for forty days, Jesus was tempted by the Devil. Why should Jesus be tempted? God must have known if Jesus was perfect and had no need to be put to the test! It is easy to read the Gospels without understanding them in depth or really thinking about their meaning, without relating the different passages to each other. Unfortunately that is no way to reach a true understanding of them.

Between the ages of twelve and thirty, then, Jesus was in India, in the Himalayas (a region influenced by Virgo: the Virgin), and there he was initiated into the great mysteries which have existed since the creation of the world. In this way he prepared himself to manifest the divine virtues of the two constellations of Virgo and Pisces: purity and abnegation.

All this is inscribed in the great book of Nature: you can find it there for yourselves. As long as a child is in its mother's womb, it is bound to her by the umbilical cord through which it receives the nourishment it needs. A mother represents Nature. When the child is separated from its mother at birth, the umbilical cord is cut. But there is another invisible cord by which every child is attached to Mother Nature who continues to give it all the nourishment it needs. This cord must not be severed until a man has been properly prepared for separate existence. If it is cut prematurely, the human being – who is still a child of Nature – will not get the nourishment he needs and will die. This invisible cord which links man to Nature, his mother, passes through the solar plexus which, as astrology tells us, is related to Virgo, the sign of the Virgin.

The two half-moon ganglia enable man to move freely in space and the five ordinary ganglia are the five loaves which nourish the multitude of cells in the human body. Each of these ganglia corresponds to one of the five virtues: goodness, justice, love, wisdom and truth. Mercury, who rules in Virgo, is the boy who brought the loaves and fishes which nourished the multitude. And the multitude are all those millions of cells of which our physical bodies are made and which, each day, are fed on the two fishes and five loaves of the solar plexus.

Many people will think that this explanation is pure fantasy and has no relation to the real miracle performed by Jesus. But I ask them, then, to refer to Chapter 16, verses 6 to 11, of St. Matthew's Gospel:

'Then Jesus said unto them, Take heed and beware of the leaven of the Pharisees and of the Saducees. And they reasoned among themselves, saying, It is because we have taken no bread. Which when Jesus perceived, he said unto them, O ye of little faith, why reason ye among yourselves, because ye have brought no bread? Do ye not yet understand, neither remember the five loaves of the five thousand, and how many baskets ye took up? Neither the seven loaves of the four thousand, and how many baskets ye took up? How is it that ye do not understand that I spake it not to you concerning bread, that ye should beware of the leaven of the Pharisees and of the Saducees?'

And in the Gospel of St. Mark (Chapter 6, verses 47 to 52), we find the following account:

'And when evening was come, the ship was in the midst of the sea, and he alone on the land. And he saw them toiling in rowing; for the wind was contrary unto them; and about the fourth watch of the night he cometh unto them, walking upon the sea, and would have passed by them. But when they saw him walking upon the sea, they supposed it had been a spirit, and cried out: For they all saw him, and were troubled. And immediately he talked with them, and saith unto them, Be of good cheer: it is I; be not afraid. And he went up unto them into the ship; and the wind ceased: and they were sore amazed in themselves beyond measure, and wondered. For they considered not the miracle of the loaves: for their heart was hardened.'

These two passages are clear evidence that:

1. The Gospel accounts of the multiplication of the loaves and fishes do not concern real, material bread and fish.

2. The miracle has some relation to Jesus' power to move freely through space (in this case he walked on water), since this power astonished his disciples who had not understood the 'miracle of the loaves'.

You should begin to see more clearly, by now, that the account of the miracle by which Jesus multiplied the loaves and fishes in order to feed thousands of people, is symbolic: it should not be taken literally. The solar plexus of every single human being feeds thousands upon thousands of cells, with its five loaves and two fishes. And there is another passage which relates to these two: 'He that believeth on me, as the scripture has said, out of his belly shall flow rivers of living water'. Here, too, Jesus was referring to the solar plexus.

If Christ is to feed the multitude of cells in our bodies, our higher consciousness has to be awakened. Everybody has a solar plexus, but most people are so bogged down in material things and their lives are so chaotic, the solar plexus cannot do its subtle work. Everybody has five loaves and two fishes but the great majority are only partially nourished: they nourish themselves physically without realizing that they should also nourish themselves on the spiritual level.

If you take these accounts literally, on the physical plane alone, you could say that Jesus did not really do anything very wonderful. One day, a very long time ago, he fed several thousand people. But what about now? All that is past and forgotten so it was not really very useful. If someone gave you a copious and delicious meal today that would not prevent you from being famished again tomorrow: you would not even remember the meal you had had today. The multitude is still with us and Jesus cannot go on feeding it physically. There are too many starving people on earth! But on the spiritual level Christ can give us the food we need every day. And we, ourselves, must imitate Christ and nourish our multitudes on a life of purity and love.

I have no physical food for you this evening: if I had, you would only want more tomorrow. What I have to give you is something far better: the means to draw on that inexhaustible supply of life for yourselves and, thereby, satisfy your hunger.

That sacred place in the Himalayas cannot be entered by one who is not pure. Our pure thoughts, feelings and acts are the only means we have of obtaining permission to enter, and those who receive this permission are those who are capable of moving freely through space and of giving their cells all the nourishment they need: they are capable of providing for their multitudes so well that twelve baskets of fragments are left over to nourish the birds and beasts of the earth.

Many people wonder why Jesus had to suffer so much in spite of being so pure and exalted, in spite of his divinity; why were the Pharisees and Saducees such bitter enemies to him and, above all, why did Judas betray him? All these things are explained by the Virgo/Pisces polarity which concerns the sixth and twelfth astrological houses. The sixth house is the house of health and sickness but also that of purity (Virgo). Jesus healed the sick with purity; he taught that there was only one way to banish demons and command the spirits and that was by prayer and fasting. Jesus cast out many devils from the sick or possessed and when the devils found themselves homeless, they sought to enter into other people, people who could provide them with the right conditions. In particular, many of them entered Pharisees and Saducees and used them to revenge themselves on Jesus. When he drove impure spirits out of the sick and possessed, Jesus was making a very great sacrifice. He was taking on himself their karmic debt: he knew he would have to suffer, he knew he would be betrayed by Judas and crucified, for the twelfth house (Pisces), is the house of trials, secret enmities and betrayals. Judas was a collective being: his role was necessary.

To the superficial observer, things in nature seem to happen haphazardly, but in fact everything is related to something else and if we do not know how things interrelate we shall never understand them. Chemistry offers a good example of this: suppose you have some pure oxygen and pure hydrogen. Even if you mix the two gases in the correct proportions in a container they will not combine to form water unless you also introduce fire (an electric spark) to trigger the reaction. The difference between chemistry and alchemy is that chemistry never mentions fire in its formulae and attributes no symbol to it as it does to other elements. Although all chemical reactions require the intervention of fire it is never mentioned in chemical formulae. For water we just say $H_2 + O = H_2O$. Chemists compose their formulae as though fire did not exist or was of no importance whereas, on the contrary, alchemy sees fire as the supreme, indispensable element, without which there can be no interaction, no result.

Oxygen is the father and hydrogen the mother and their offspring, water, looks like neither of its parents! Oxygen represents the masculine and hydrogen the feminine principle and, together, they produce water. This is simply an image. In man, oxygen is the intellect and hydrogen the heart. The intellect is one thing and the heart quite another, and they can live side by side in the same 'container' without ever combining. But if they do not combine they cannot produce water... and water signifies life. Nowadays, this lack of unity between the heart and the intellect is visible in so many areas: in families, where husband and wife are disunited; in society where intellectuals and men of sentiment are constantly at loggerheads, and, above all, in each human being whose thoughts and feelings pull in opposite directions. In order for heart and mind to combine in unity, fire is needed: the fire of love. And when heart and mind are united by the fire of love they produce a child, an action, the fruit of their union and of the harmonious balance that reigns in their relationship. When minds and hearts unite they produce water, the symbol of life. Acting in and through the masculine and feminine principles, fire produces water. This is just one demonstration of that great truth expressed by Initiates: Love gives birth to Life; Life is the child of Love. Unless your mind and heart combine and pull the same way you will produce no water and you will dry up.

A great many nervous diseases are caused by the divergence between men's hearts and minds. Modern medicine can say what it likes about nervous disorders, but the principal cause is simple: it is that rift between heart and mind. Make every effort to unite your own hearts and minds and you will see for yourselves how happy you will be when they act as one. Where there is water, where there is life, we can be sure that the two principles are united and working harmoniously together.

And all the family and social problems of the day are only a reflection of what exists in human souls: people are united, but only on the outside. For a true family and a true society to exist, there must be that element of fire to unite the members and water to give them life.

Paris, May 14, 1938

7

The Feet and the Solar Plexus

'Now before the feast of the passover, when Jesus knew that his hour was come that he should depart out of this world unto the Father, having loved his own which were in the world, he loved them unto the end. And supper being ended, the devil having now put into the heart of Judas Iscariot, Simon's son, to betray him; Jesus knowing that the Father had given all things into his hands, and that he was come from God, and went to God; He riseth from supper, and laid aside his garments; and took a towel, and girded himself. After that he poureth water into a basin, and began to wash the disciples' feet, and to wipe them with the towel wherewith he was girded. Then cometh he to Simon Peter: and Peter saith unto him, Lord dost thou wash my feet? Jesus answered and said unto him, What I do thou knowest not now; but thou shalt know hereafter. Peter saith unto him, Thou shalt never wash my feet. Jesus answered him, If I wash thee not thou hast no part with me. Simon Peter saith unto him, Lord not my feet only, but also my hands and my head. Jesus saith to him, He that is washed needeth not save to wash his feet, but is clean every whit: and ye are clean, but not all.'

John 13: 1-10

The passage I have just read to you is very well-known: everyone is always much struck with this gesture Jesus made during his last meal with his disciples. Traditionally, it has been interpreted as a lesson of humility that Jesus wanted to give his disciples, and this is absolutely correct, but it is not complete. So, today, if you have no objection, I propose to give you some additional explanations which are very important for your spiritual evolution. It all depends, though, on how you take these explanations. If I gave you a seed, telling you that it possessed miraculous properties, and you threw it away or left it in a cupboard instead of planting and watering it, how could it sprout and grow? People are always in a hurry, they don't take the time to wait and see how the seeds they have sown are sprouting and what kind of fruit they will bear. So what you get out of this lecture will depend entirely on you. Those who listen with the desire to benefit from all they hear will certainly find all kinds of treasures in it.

Jesus left the table, therefore, took a cloth and began to wash his disciples' feet. To begin with, St. Peter would not let his Master wash his feet, and Jesus told him that he did not understand what he was doing, now, but that he would understand later. We can presume, therefore, that Jesus had the intention of explaining this gesture to his disciples, as he had explained many other things to them, although these explanations have never been found in the Gospel account. At the end of his Gospel, St. John says: 'And there are also many other things which Jesus did, the which, if they should be written every one, I suppose that even the world itself could not contain the books that should be written'.

A lot of people suppose that the disciples were men of no education or intelligence. But this is not so: Jesus chose them because they had been Initiates and Magi in the past. No one can become the disciple of a great Master if he has not earned the privilege, if he has not worked to cultivate the necessary qualities and virtues in past lives. Even the most incredulous of Jesus' disciples, Thomas, was a reincarnation of Solomon and he was happy to be Jesus' humble disciple. And if you don't believe me... go and find out for yourselves!

It is the same thing for Jesus: a lot of religious people do not believe he was learned. They think he could perform miracles without ever having studied and worked to prepare himself. But the Gospels reveal nothing of what Jesus did between the ages of twelve and thirty. Where did he disappear to for eighteen years? The answer can be found in the archives of the Universal White Brotherhood, where his life is recorded in detail: here we learn that Jesus travelled during that period and that he went to the Himalayas where he was initiated by great Initiates.

Contemporary science studies the phenomena of nature in a very inadequate way: it fails to take into account the relationship between different phenomena. But Jesus knew the relationship between the different parts of our bodies and the phenomena of nature and we, too, must know about this if we are to understand why Jesus washed his disciples' feet.

When I explained the miracle of the multiplication of the five loaves and two fishes with which Jesus fed 5,000 people, I talked about certain astrological correspondences between the feet and the solar plexus. Jesus was born just at the time when the vernal point was entering the constellation of Pisces. And the Christian era is under the sign of Pisces and its polar opposite, Virgo. Jesus was born of the Virgin and he, himself, represents Pisces, the fish. Today we shall be talking about the Pisces/Virgo polarity again, but from another point of view.

As I told you, therefore, in the human body the feet correspond to the constellation of Pisces (fish), and the solar plexus to that of Virgo (virgin). Jesus washed his disciples' feet in order to show them the very important relationship between the feet and the solar plexus. Today I shall talk to you in some detail about the solar plexus and the sympathetic nerve-system of which it is a part.

The sympathetic nervous system consists of a double chain of ganglia and nerves, running from the brain down either side of the spinal cord to its base in the lumbar region. The various nerves and ganglia form complex interlacing networks known as plexuses: the solar plexus is one of these.

If you will now refer to the diagrams shown in figures 12 and 13, you will see how the ganglia of the sympathetic system are grouped:

– Three pairs of cranial ganglia lying along the trigeminal nerve;

– Three pairs of cervical ganglia connected to the heart;

– Twelve pairs of dorsal ganglia connected to the lungs and the solar plexus;

– Four pairs of lumbar ganglia connected, also, to the solar plexus and, through it, to the stomach, small intestine, liver, pancreas and kidneys;

– Four pairs of sacral ganglia connected to the rectum, the genital organs and the bladder.

This gives twenty-six pairs in all, and this figure is no accident: it is the sum of the four letters composing the sacred name of God הוהי, in which י = 10, ה = 5, ו = 6, ה = 5. The name of God is based on the same laws that determine the structure of the human sympathetic nervous system.

The two groups of three pairs of ganglia, cranial and cervical, correspond to the divine world, the psychological dimension of nature, the Caballah.

The twelve pairs of dorsal ganglia correspond to the spiritual dimension; they represent the physiological aspect of nature, astrology.

The two groups of four pairs of lumbar and sacral ganglia are in relation to the physical dimension; they correspond to the anatomical aspect of nature, alchemy.

Figure 14 illustrates this more clearly.

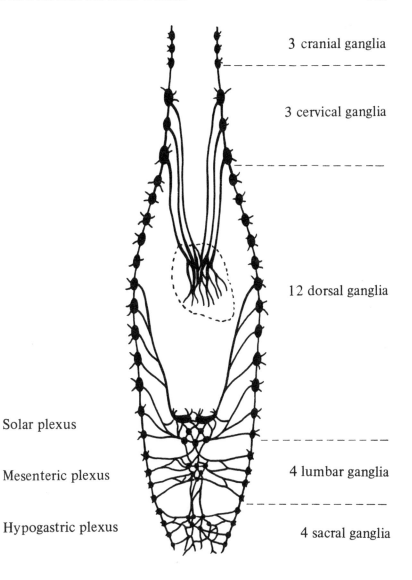

3 cranial ganglia

3 cervical ganglia

12 dorsal ganglia

Solar plexus

Mesenteric plexus

Hypogastric plexus

4 lumbar ganglia

4 sacral ganglia

Chain of ganglia in the sympathetic nerve-system
Figure 12

There are two sets of three pairs of ganglia (cranial and cervical), and Three is the divine number, the number of the Caballah which reveals the principles at work in the universe. The Caballah answers the question, 'Who?': Who created? Who is at work in the universe? Who permits...?

Then we have twelve pairs of dorsal ganglia: Twelve is the number of Nature and of astrology (twelve constellations of the Zodiac) which studies the influence of the heavenly bodies, the functions of the organs of the cosmic body. Astrology corresponds to the circulatory and respiratory systems. The vernal point, for example, retrogrades one degree every seventy-two years and the human heart beats seventy-two times a minute. Also, we normally breathe in and out eighteen times a minute, and eighteen is a quarter of seventy-two. Astrology answers the question, 'When?'

There are two sets of four pairs of ganglia (lumbar and sacral), and Four is the alchemists' number; the four states of matter: earth, water, air and fire. Alchemy replies to the question 'What?'

The sympathetic nervous system has an important role to play in the human body:

1. By means of the sensory fibres which connect the nutritional organs to the gray matter of the spinal cord, and

2. By means of its motor fibres which connect the gray matter to the smooth tissues of the internal organs and to the muscle fibres of heart and glands.

The sympathetic system controls the mechanisms of digestion, respiration, circulation and excretion and these functions all occur, normally speaking, without our conscious knowledge. Some Initiates, however, manage to control the sympathetic system and, thereby, the organs governed by it. For a very long time it was believed that there was no direct connection between the brain and the sympathetic system, but science now knows that it is all linked together.

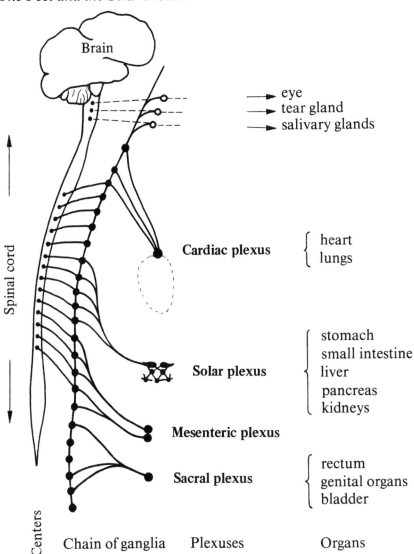

Diagram illustrating the sympathetic system
Figure 13

The brain cannot act directly on the internal organs, however; its orders have to be transmitted through the sympathetic system. Initiates work at making the link between the solar plexus and the brain conscious, for once it has been raised to the level of consciousness, everything becomes easy.* There are yogis in India and elsewhere who have practised working with the solar plexus for a very long time and who have mastered the art of healing a wound, made by themselves or someone else, very rapidly.

As you have noticed, the twenty-six ganglia of the sympathetic system are divided into five groups. These five groups are related to the five virtues: purity, justice, love, wisdom and truth.

– Purity is linked to the four pairs of sacral ganglia which constitute the base of the chain of ganglia, for purity is the base or foundation.**

– Justice is related to the four pairs or lumbar ganglia (which are located near the kidneys, and the kidneys are related to Libra, the symbol of balance or equilibrium) and to the organs of nutrition: stomach, liver, intestine, etc. When a man does not nourish himself correctly the balance is upset and the ensuing problems reveal that justice is taking steps to restore order.

– Love is related to the twelve pairs of dorsal ganglia. Love is a force which causes us to expand (and expansion can be seen in the act of breathing) and which unites us to all creatures, to the whole universe represented by the twelve constellations of the Zodiac.

– Wisdom is linked to the three pairs of cervical ganglia, for true wisdom comes from the heart.

* In this connection, see the following lectures, 'Night and Day – the Conscious and the Subconscious', vol 10, and 'The Five Wise Virgins and the Five Foolish Virgins', vol 3.

** See vol. 7, 'The Mysteries of Yesod'.

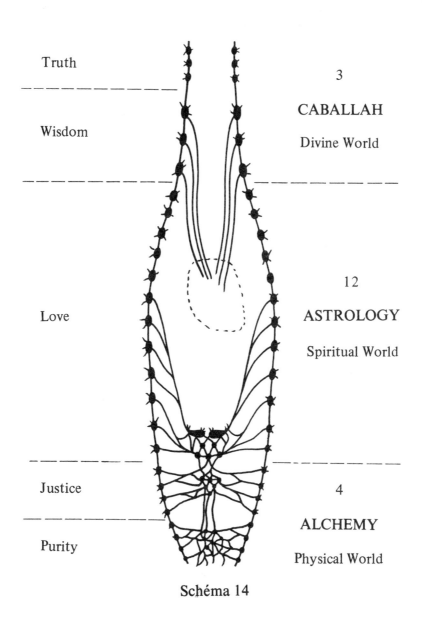

Truth	
	3
Wisdom	**CABALLAH**
	Divine World
Love	12
	ASTROLOGY
	Spiritual World
Justice	4
	ALCHEMY
Purity	Physical World

Schéma 14

– Truth is linked to the three pairs of cranial ganglia, for truth is above everything else; it is the summit, the goal.

Truth, wisdom, love, justice and purity put us in contact with all the harmonious forces of the universe whose blessings we receive. Each virtue improves the functioning of the ganglia and organs to which it is related, just as a fault against one of these virtues impairs that functioning.

A very close link exists between psychic and physical states. When we are sad, for instance, our condition acts on the sympathetic system and triggers the vasoconstrictor function which contracts the arteries. The result is that one feels poor, alone and abandoned. It may not be true at all, but it is the impression one has. So the contraction triggered by sadness prevents the blood from circulating properly and, consequently, also hampers one's digestion, one's breathing, etc. To relax the nerves one has to call on joy and love: every day, when you get up, instead of thinking, 'Oh me, oh my! I've got no money, my sweetheart is unfaithful, I haven't received the letters I was expecting, etc., etc.', you should do your utmost to cultivate positive thoughts. Every morning, when he gets up, the disciple's thoughts are of gratitude: 'Lord God, Creator of all things, I thank you because I am alive and well, because I can breathe, walk about, sing, see and hear... what invaluable treasures are these!' We should get up in the morning joyfully and with a heart full of gratitude to the Lord. If human beings grow old so quickly it is because they have no idea how to flavour their lives with joy every day.

But now let us get back to the account of how Jesus washed his disciples' feet. By his gesture he was saying, 'This is an example I am giving you. Later on too you will have to show the same humility and the same disinterestedness towards others'. Jesus even washed Judas' feet although he knew that Judas had already betrayed him. Symbolically, someone who refuses to revenge himself on those who have injured him, washes their feet.

But the principal meaning behind Jesus' gesture in washing his disciples' feet was to awaken the constructive forces in the solar plexus. It is more than likely that, in the ordinary circumstances of your lives, you have noticed the link between the feet and the solar plexus. If you had cold feet, for instance, you may have been aware of a certain tenseness in the solar plexus and if you ate when you felt like that you will probably have had indigestion! Whereas if you start by having a hot footbath, you will feel the plexus relaxing, which gives you a warm, pleasant feeling and puts you in a good humour!

When you have to face a very painful situation or meet someone you dislike, your solar plexus tightens up and you feel out of humour. But if you meet someone you are fond of or see something lovely (a waterfall, a mountain, a garden full of flowers) you feel expansive. Why?

Obviously not everybody feels these reactions or, at least, not everybody is aware of them. Not everybody is capable of feeling and analyzing what goes on in their solar plexus. But disciples of a spiritual teaching must become more and more sensitive and more and more conscious and capable of observing what goes on inside them. In this way they discover many interesting things. The solar plexus becomes their guide; it gives them all kinds of information about all kinds of people and things. People sometimes speak of a sixth sense: that sixth sense is the solar plexus.

The solar plexus is an extremely important centre for us and we must avoid whatever makes it tense, because this leads to the contraction of the blood vessels and other tracts and canals in the body. And when the blood or other body fluids cannot circulate properly, waste products are deposited on the walls of the vessels and lead, in the long run, to serious health problems.

The things that most disturb the plexus (and, consequently, also the internal organs: liver, kidneys, stomach, etc.) are fear, anger, worry, doubt and immoderate love. Chaotic thoughts and emotions destroy the harmony of the solar plexus and as it is the reservoir of life forces, the result of this disharmony is a total loss of all one's magnetic force. When you have a shock or a sudden fright you find yourself without an ounce of strength; your legs give way beneath you, your hands tremble and your mind is paralyzed. This means that your solar plexus has been drained of all its strength.

So, the solar plexus can be emptied, but it can also be filled and it is this that the disciple has to learn: how to fill his solar plexus. I shall give you some different methods.

A tree is a reservoir of forces that it has received both from the sun and from the earth, and we can draw on these forces. Choose a big, strong tree: an oak, beech or pine, for instance. Stand with your back up against it and with your left hand between the tree and your back, the palm pressing on the tree trunk; at the same time place the palm of your right hand on your plexus. Concentrate your thoughts on the tree, asking it to give you some of its strength, which you will receive through your left hand and transmit to your solar plexus with the right hand. It is a kind of energy-transfusion.

You can also strengthen your solar plexus by watching and listening to running water: a fountain, a spring or a waterfall. These methods are so simple they seem insignificant, but they produce very good results. Running water influences the solar plexus which sets to work to expel harmful elements. We often watch running water but without realizing the use we could make of it so it does not produce any great results.

You can also plunge your hands – or better still, your feet – into water. When you feel that you have lost your magnetic force, when you are troubled or tense, prepare a basin of hot water, consciously, plunge your feet into the water and wash them with conscious attention. In this way you can influence your solar plexus and reinforce it, and your state of mind will immediately be transformed. If you find you cannot meditate one day, have a footbath and you will see that it will suddenly be much easier to concentrate. It is not necessary to keep your feet in the water for long, but you can talk to them as you wash them gently, saying, 'My dear feet, I'm just beginning to understand how well you serve me. I never pay any attention to you and yet you bear my weight and take me wherever I want to go. From now on I shall be more grateful for all your patience and humility.'

Certain cells have been sent to work in the feet in order to learn something: it is a school and a testing ground for them. They are living beings, these cells, and one day they are going to have to pass a test. If they do well, Cosmic Intelligence will tell them, 'Now you can move up', and they will move to the lungs, the heart or the brain in order to continue their evolution. If they have been sent to your feet, at the moment, it is because they need to learn humility and kindness which they lacked in the past.

The same pattern can be seen in the lives of men: destiny condemns all those who have been hard-headed, proud and vicious to be born into peoples or families who have to suffer in order to learn the laws of justice, humility and sacrifice. Thus speaks Initiatic Science, whether we believe it or not.

Every single cell has to evolve. The most advanced are those of the heart. Whereas other cells sleep, amuse themselves or rest, the cells of the heart are ceaselessly at work to sustain the whole body and give it the strength it needs. Cells are beings which have to work together for the good of the whole. When some of them want to free themselves and form a separate kingdom, then a serious illness afflicts the body. But if our cells sometimes break away from the harmony of the whole it is not their fault. It is man himself who is guilty;

it is he who gives them the bad example, so it is he who is responsible. Illness is the result of our thoughts, feelings and actions which indirectly affect our sympathetic nerve-system.

In the future, science will teach men to live harmoniously, which means, first and foremost, to know how to make use of whatever reinforces the solar plexus. Look at how many people love to contemplate the setting sun or falling autumn leaves, and wallow in melancholy thoughts and memories of lost loves, etc. You must avoid this kind of thing; a disciple must ally himself only to what is living, rising and waxing in nature, to all that can illuminate, strengthen and elevate him. Whatever we experience in life, whatever we eat, breathe or touch affects our solar plexus, and this is why there are things we should never touch, nor eat, nor listen to, nor look at, because they have a debilitating effect on the plexus. By contrast, if we watch the sun rising in the morning we can feel something rising within us. And if we go outdoors in spring, when everything is bursting into leaf and bud and flower, we shall feel that something begins to burst into flower within us, too.

But let's get back to why our feet are so important. We should never forget that it is by means of our feet that we are in touch with the earth and its currents. The feet are like antennae. I once had a friend who could tell from his toes when there was going to be heavy rain or a thunderstorm. He knew it a long time in advance: he was a perfect meteorological office! But the electric and magnetic currents which flow in and out of the earth will only normally circulate through one's feet if they are not prevented from doing so by layers of dust or fluids; this is why it is a good idea to wash one's feet every evening.

You remember that, to begin with, Peter did not want Jesus to wash his feet. Then, later, he wanted him to wash his head and his hands as well, but Jesus said, 'He that is washed needeth not save to wash his feet, but is clean every whit'.

The feet, being the part of the body which is most closely in contact with the earth, represent the physical plane from which we have to free ourselves in order to gain access to the higher planes. This is why, if we concentrate our conscious attention on the centres beneath and on top of our feet while we wash them, we can work towards this liberation from the physical plane. Have you ever thought about why the Greek God Hermes was represented with wings on his heels? Hermes was the messenger of the gods and the wings symbolized his power to move freely through space. But Hermes' wings should also be interpreted as representing the chakras, or centres, of the feet. If these centres are awakened they will enable man to move freely in space and to reach the subtler planes.

Remember what I told you about the solar plexus in my lecture about the miracle of the five loaves and two fishes: this miracle is related to Jesus' power to displace himself at will. St. Mark makes this clear when, after telling about how Jesus walked on the waters to come to the disciples' aid during the storm, he said: 'And they were sore amazed in themselves beyond measure, and wondered, for they had not understood the miracle of the loaves'. So, here again, you can see that this correspondence between the feet and the solar plexus is related to the possibility of moving freely in space.

As I mentioned: the feet are related to the physical plane and it is on this plane that we are always victims because the physical plane is always more or less closely connected to the subterranean, diabolical world. The feet are seen, symbolically, as man's most vulnerable spot for this reason. And there is another myth, the myth of Achilles, that expresses this. Achilles' mother, wanting to render him invulnerable, plunged him into the waters of the river Styx, holding him by his heel which, therefore, was not immersed like the rest of his body, and Achilles died from the wound of a poisoned arrow which struck him in the heel.

Now you can better understand Jesus' gesture and his words, when he washed his disciples' feet and told Peter, 'He that is washed needeth not save to wash his feet, but is clean every whit'. Since our feet represent the physical, most material plane, to wash our feet means the ultimate purification.

There are a great many more things which could be said about the feet. From time immemorial, the wise men of the world have known about the correspondences between the microcosmos and the macrocosmos and this science of correspondences reveals not only that the different parts of man's body correspond to different constellations of the Zodiac (the head is related to Aries, the neck to Taurus, etc.), but that each part stands in relation to the whole body, to the whole universe and to the powers and qualities of the soul. These relationships have been studied for the hands, but they exist also for the feet. There are certain precise spots on the feet which are related to other organs of the body, so that if you work on these spots you can cure certain anomalies in the other organs.

But, this evening, what I wanted to show you was that when Jesus washed his disciples' feet, his gesture had a much deeper and more far-reaching significance than is normally realized. Think about all I have told you, begin to work on your feet and your solar plexus on the spiritual level, and you will soon experience the blessings that these methods can bring you.

May light and peace be with you!

Paris, March 18, 1939

8

The Parable of the Tares

'Another parable put he forth unto them, saying, The kingdom of heaven is likened unto a man which sowed good seed in his field: but while men slept, his enemy came and sowed tares among the wheat, and went his way. But when the blade was sprung up, and brought forth fruit, then appeared the tares also. So the servants of the householder came and said unto him, Sir, didst not thou sow good seed in thy field? From whence then hath it tares? He said unto them, An enemy hath done this. The servants said unto him: Wilt thou then that we go and gather them up? But he said, Nay; lest while ye gather up the tares, ye root up also the wheat with them. Let both grow together until the harvest: and in the time of harvest I will say to the reapers, Gather ye together first the tares, and bind them in bundles to burn them: but gather the wheat into my barn.'

Matthew 13 : 24-30

Jesus often used images of fields, the sower, seeds, etc. in his parables and as he explained them himself, there is no need for me to discuss them again. Today I am interested only in the reply the householder gave his servants when they asked him if they should pull out the weeds from among the wheat. He said, 'Nay, lest while ye gather up the tares, ye root up also the wheat with them. Let both grow together until the harvest.'

To begin with, let us look at the question of the wheat and the tares. These are symbols of realities that exist not only in the vegetable kingdom but also amongst animals and birds, in human society and in our own structure. Wheat, an essential food for human beings, and tares, a weed which hinders the free growth of the cereal crops, are two symbols which can be found in different forms in all areas.

It is probable that tares* contain elements which could be useful to man. There are a great many herbs, plants and fruits that science neglected for a long time until, one fine day, it was discovered that they contained some element which could be used to cure certain illnesses, or in manufacturing some other product. None of the elements in Nature's great laboratory is useless.

If you understand this parable of the wheat and the tares, you will have understood one of the most important laws of life: how to keep on growing and improving in spite of apparently unfavourable conditions allotted to us by fate; how to abide by the rule given by the householder: 'Let both grow together until the harvest'. This is an extremely important question from the pedagogical and social points of view. People are always crying out against evil and evildoers, against the vices of society; time and again one hears such expressions as, 'Root them out! Let's get rid of them! They should be done away with! Hang them!' etc. But humanity has never, since the beginning of the world, managed to get rid of evil or evildoers.

Every day you are obliged to live shoulder to shoulder with detestable people who, from your point of view, are like the tares, and you ask nothing better than to get rid of them.

* Also known as Rye-grass or Ray-grass, a type of vetch. (Translator's note)

But would that be the best solution? Is there no better method than that of violence and destruction? People believe that if only they could do away with the wicked they would be able to live in peace. But that is exactly like trying to get rid of mosquitos without drying out the swamps in which they breed. To get rid of evil it is not enough to get rid of those who do evil, for they are the product of certain conditions. It is the conditions that have to be changed, therefore; if you dry out the swamps there will be no more mosquitos. You tell me that you know all that, and I don't doubt it, but what you do not realize is that you too have a swamp inside you which is a breeding ground for evil and evildoers. You spend your whole time killing the mosquitos that are bothering you, but you do nothing about drying out your swamp. And this is so true of all of us!

Just observe the reactions of the educational and religious leaders and moralists. Their vocabulary is filled with expressions such as 'Let us uproot our vices! Let us eliminate our bad habits!' That is a very commendable intention, no doubt, but how does one set about it? All these people have weapons for the extermination of evil but that does not seem to prevent it from flourishing. In fact some people who have been freed from certain vices become the prey of even worse vices still.

The interpretation that is usually given of this parable is that the field represents the world and the wheat and tares represent the good and the wicked respectively, and that one day they will be separated. This is correct but it is incomplete. The wheatfield represents not only the world, but the individual man also, for each one of us has both wheat and tares growing in us. In other words we all have our better and our lower natures. We may sometimes wonder how it is that man, who was created in the image of God and whom the Creator endowed with His own divine qualities, should manifest such bizarre tendencies and the desire to lie, steal, kill and betray. How is it possible that God should be the Creator of a vicious criminal? The parable answers this question. It says that an enemy came while we were asleep and sowed seeds in us of another nature than those we had received from God, with the result that both kinds of seeds sprout and grow in us, together. It is the words, 'While men slept' that explain every-thing. And this can happen even to the most highly advanced beings. When one's consciousness falls asleep, one's intelli-gence becomes clouded and the enemy (which stands for an assemblage of many, many very inferior beings who pursue goals contrary to the evolutionary order) sows his thoughts, feelings and desires in the human soul. This is why the disci-ples of the Universal White Brotherhood must learn to be very watchful and very wakeful, even in their sleep: even when the body sleeps the soul must never fall asleep.

Ever since the beginning of the world, tares have been an object of much study by men. In hospitals, schools and courts of law, men attempt to analyze the elements that make up tares, but evil cannot always be clearly distinguished in all its manifestations. Good and evil are so tightly interwoven, that if one tries to uproot one there is every likelihood that the other will be uprooted at the same time. The only thing to do is to separate them, as Hermes Trismegistus advised, saying, 'You shall separate the subtle from the gross with great dili-gence'.

Man still does not have the knowledge or the capacity to get rid of evil, so the best solution is to let good and evil live side by side and to use the activity and the extraordinarily powerful forces contained in the elements of evil, that is to say, to take infinitely small doses of evil to reinforce and stim-ulate the forces of good. Exactly like a graft: what does the nurseryman do when he wants to increase his pear crop? He grafts a small branch of a good quality pear tree onto a vigor-ous young wild pear with bitter, inedible fruit, and the branch benefits from all the strength and energy of the wild tree. In the same way we can graft the branches of good onto the tree of evil. Just as the forces of evil take advantage of the forces of good to draw strength from them and use them to their own, evil ends, so must the forces of good learn to exercise their right to draw strength from the forces of evil and transform them to their own ends.

We all have organs whose functions do not seem either particularly spiritual or aesthetic but which are, nevertheless, extremely important: we should never try to get rid of them. And we must realize that, in nature, every single thing is in some way bound to another: every cell, every organ is bound to other cells, other organs, just as the roots of a tree are connected to the branches, the leaves, the flowers and the fruit. If man cuts off his roots, in other words if he eliminates the organs which constitute the foundation of his existence, he will suffer most terrible consequences. It is true that, sometimes, these organs are the cause of tragedies, but he must let them live and try to draw strength from them and transform them.

If you read the biography of some remarkable man, it is often quite amazing to see how he had many abnormal, even criminal, monstrous tendencies in his make-up; and this is true of many great men. When one does not understand how man is built, it seems that this is an impossible contradiction, but in point of fact the explanation is simple: these men constantly resisted and struggled to overcome their baser tendencies and, thanks to this struggle, whether they knew it or not, they grafted good onto evil. The more daunting, the more ardent were their passions (their roots), the sweeter and more delectable were their fruits, the more remarkable their achievements. A great many other people, who had none of those hideous defects contributed nothing to mankind either, and lived mediocre, insignificant lives.

I am not saying that we should tolerate, justify or cultivate evil in the world: no! But we must try to understand that sublime philosophy that teaches how to use everything, even the forces of evil for the glory of good. The taller the trunk and the greater the branches of a tree, the deeper its roots. Someone who does not understand this is appalled by the all-pervasiveness of evil. You must not be afraid: everything in nature is constructed according to most marvellous laws. If our roots are not deep we shall be unable to draw life from the ground.

Nature is unutterably wiser than we. We think that snake venom, for instance, is evil because it can be a deadly poison. And yet there are learned people who collect adders' venom and other poisonous substances and who cure certain diseases with them. Poison is a highly concentrated substance which, if taken undiluted, the body cannot tolerate, but if you know what dose to give, it can save lives. Similarly, those of you who live close to evil people must try and understand that they possess some highly concentrated forces which, if diluted, can be very useful. All the work of a disciple consists in learning how to use these forces, how to measure the perfect dose.

It is very dangerous to venture into the philosophical study of the origins and present existence of evil, particularly if one spends all one's energies on that. Nobody has ever been able to eliminate evil and all those who have tried to fight evil without being in possession of the true science have always been the losers. Only the great Archangels and Gods can solve the problem of evil. You should not concern yourselves with evil nor even try to fight it: you should concern yourselves only with good, for that is the only way to transform evil, by drawing strength from it. You must learn to put evil to work for the benefit of the forces of good: love, wisdom and truth. But only he who possesses purity in his heart, wisdom in his intellect, love in his soul and truth in his spirit can transform and improve everything.

So don't worry about evil; let the tares grow alongside the wheat for how can you uproot the tares without damaging the wheat at the same time? Tares grow in every family, in every society: how can you weed out the husband without harming the wife (or vice versa) when they are so closely bound to each other and refuse to be separated? It would take an extremely skilful surgeon to cut out only the diseased part of an organ and leave the healthy cells whole and intact. It takes a good dentist to draw only the one, rotten tooth! It takes a highly experienced judge to punish the guilty without harming the innocent, as so often happens today.

Besides, ask the learned scholars and professors if they would like you to do away with the ignorant. They would protest vociferously, saying that you would be doing them a very bad turn because then they would have no one to teach and to dazzle with all their science! What would all the doctors and pharmacists (chemists) do if there were no more sick people, no more diseases? They would all starve to death. What would businessmen do if there were no more gullible victims for them to fleece? They would protest, 'Let the tares go on growing amongst us so that we can exploit them'.

Now, let us pause for a moment to consider what the householder said to his workers: 'In the time of harvest I will say to the reapers, Gather ye together first the tares, and bind them in bundles to burn them'. So you see, the tares end by being thrown on the fire. We free ourselves from our gangue by passing through fire seven times, for only fire can separate good from evil. When you have a fever, what is happening? Harvest time is there. It is, no doubt, a very small harvest (the final harvest would certainly have been harder to bear and who knows if you would have been gathered into the granary or thrown on the fire to burn?). When the fire (the fever) is on you it melts the tares in you and burns them up. In other words it eliminates the evil in you and all those waste materials that prevent you from growing. When the fire has done its work you sigh with relief because you feel better. So there are large and small harvests and fever comes to help us get rid of certain tares. Tares exist on the three levels: physical, astral and mental.

There is a marvellous flow of exchange between the good and the wicked. On the face of the earth there are mountains and there are plains, and certain currents flow between them, producing certain manifestations of life. If the earth were completely flat there would be no life. Jesus, who was well aware of this law, was always to be found amongst the poor, sinners and criminals, whereas the Pharisees and Saducees, who were ignorant of the laws of nature, despised Jesus and accused him of frequenting the ignorant, sinful masses. Their pride kept them apart from the poor and disinherited whereas Jesus preferred to live amongst those who were weak and ill or who had fallen on evil times, in order to set up a flow of exchange with them. He gave them his light, love and purity in exchange for the raw, unrefined materials he drew from them, just as the roots of a tree draws its sustenance from the raw materials of the earth, thus enabling the tree to produce flowers and fruit. The wicked supply the energy and the good absorb, transform and distribute it in the form of finished products: kindness, charity, understanding. This exchange is necessary. Jesus took on himself the sins of men: this means that he drew raw energy from them and transformed it in the leaves of his being so as to redistribute it in the form of light and love.

He who refuses to have anything to do with the ignorant and the wicked and who frequents only those who are well-mannered, learned and virtuous, will never evolve very far because he is no alchemist: he deprives himself of certain qualities and virtues which he needs in order to evolve. This is why, in spite of all their learning, the Pharisees were ignorant for they kept themselves apart from the masses... although this did not prevent them from being even more sinful and vicious than those they despised! Whereas, on the contrary, Jesus descended as far as it is possible to go; he mixed freely with the masses, but he did so consciously, working to instruct and purify them and raise them up to God. The Pharisees' mistrust and pride laid their souls wide open to impurities and weakness, whereas Jesus' boldness, conviction and love purified the air around him wherever he went.

I am not saying this with the intention of encouraging you to frequent all the degenerates and malefactors you can find. Before you go anywhere near them you must begin by making a very careful study of the question of the wheat and the tares, in other words you must have learned how to transmute evil into good as I have just explained. I have sometimes known of some charming, virtuous women who have married drunken and debauched men in the hope of saving them, but the desire to rescue someone from his own vices is not enough; instead of saving their husbands it is they who were debased and dishonoured. Knowledge is necessary before one can transform evil into good. Initiates can help us because they take on themselves our sins, errors and weaknesses and, in exchange, they give us their light, peace and love. Only Initiates have this indispensable knowledge that enables them to transmute evil into good: only they know what virtues tares contain and are capable of using them. But I am not allowed to talk to you about this, for you are not yet capable of using the precious elements contained in tares.

But this exchange that Initiates are able to operate with the masses is also going on constantly in us, in the depths of our being. The stomach, for instance, is a factory in which raw materials are transformed; this is where we find the roots of our physical being. The raw material which has been fed to the stomach is further refined and elaborated in the lungs, the heart and the brain, becoming thoughts and emotions which then in turn, penetrate throughout the body to nourish the cells with their subtle energies. This is how that on-going exchange between our lower and our higher natures is effected. Without it, without a permanent circulation of energies we would die.

St. Paul wrote, 'There was given to me a thorn in the flesh... I besought the Lord thrice, that it might depart from me. And He said unto me, My grace is sufficient for thee: for my strength is made perfect in weakness'. He who has a weakness of soul or body tries to cure it without realizing that that weakness can be a source of great grace. If men always enjoyed ideal conditions in which all their desires were fulfilled everything would come to a standstill within them because they would not be spurred on by pain and they would stagnate. It is our imperfections, the thorns in our flesh that force us to work in depth and to try to come ever closer to Heaven and to God. Sometimes Heaven leaves us with our weaknesses in order to stimulate us to work on the spiritual level; for an apparent weakness is, in fact, a strength, a potential. If our spirit and intellect are enlightened, we can use these weaknesses, these desires and instincts which torment us. They are laboratories in which we can work every day to extract energies and materials and learn to become great alchemists.

So cheer up! You are all very well off because you all have weaknesses; but it is essential that you learn to use them and put them to work for good. We have to put our baser tendencies to work just as the forces of nature have been harnessed and put to work: the winds, waterfalls, fire, electricity, heat and light. People take it for granted that we can use the forces of nature, but if one talks to them about harnessing the winds and storms, the waterfalls or the thunderbolts that are in them, they are astonished. And yet, nothing could be more natural: once you know the rules of spiritual alchemy you will know how to transform and make use of the energies within you.

Let's refer, once again, to the diagram we have already studied several times : it is a key to the secret doors of nature and our own souls.

This evening, however, we shall study it from a slightly different point of view.

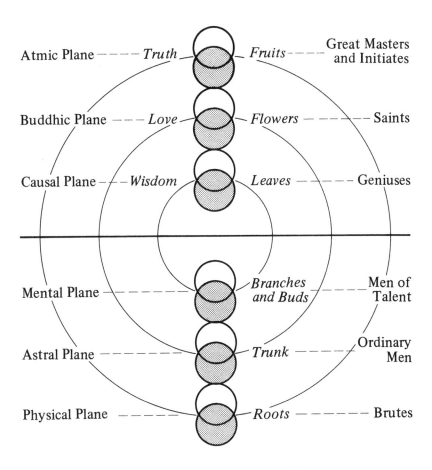

Figure 1

The first thing to notice is that it represents the different types of men: brutes (which correspond to the physical plane), ordinary people (astral plane), men of talent (mental plane), geniuses (causal plane), saints (buddhic plane) and great Masters (atmic plane).

Now, let's compare these different human types with the different parts of a tree. The brutes are in the roots of life, they work underground. Ordinary people work in the trunk of the tree, and the raw materials that others will transform, on a higher level, pass through their hands. The talented represent the branches which pass on the raw materials to the leaves and, once it has been transformed, pass it back towards the base of the tree. The branches take, therefore, in order to give to humanity; their function is to exchange. Geniuses are the leaf-buds; this is where the Great Work begins: the transmutation of the raw sap through the action of the sun's rays. The saints are the flowers of the Cosmic Tree; by their colour, their perfume and their beauty, they attract butterflies and insects, birds and human beings. They are predestined to form the fruits: thanks to their work, life becomes pure and beautiful. And the great Masters are the fruits of the Cosmic Tree; they are the bread of God, the 'bread from Heaven'. In them is the sweet savour of every quintessence.

A human being represents a tree with its roots, trunk, branches, leaves, flowers and fruit. All men have roots, a trunk and branches but very few receive the kiss of spring: most of them are barren. They bear no fruit nor flowers nor even leaves: they are mournful winter trees, black and stark. And yet every single human being has a lotus blossom within him. But it takes a great deal of work and understanding as well as the sacrifice of a great deal of time to induce these flowers to bloom, to perfume the air with their fragrance and to form fruit. The fruits are the accomplishments of the different virtues.

In India, the concept of the birth of the divinity is symbolized by the lotus blossom in which Krishna is born. The birth of Krishna is the birth of one's higher Self, Christ, within one. But there is also the myth that tells how Saturn was overthrown by his son, Jupiter, and took refuge underground where he works in the mines, and this myth expresses man's fall to the lowest, most dense material level, the level of roots, and on this level light and movement are severly restricted. The higher one moves up the trunk and into the branches and leaves, the freer one is to move about and the more light, warmth and joy one finds.

Leaves, flowers, fruit: these are love, wisdom and truth. Leaves represent wisdom, flowers represent love and fruit represent truth. The leaves show immense wisdom when they transform the raw sap, just as alchemists transformed base metals into gold with the help of the Philosopher's Stone. The flowers are associated with love: their colours and perfumes and the fragile purity of their petals are an attraction for all creatures. It is the flowers which contain the nectar that insects feed on. Fruits represent truth, the result of the union of wisdom and love.

At certain seasons of the year a tree is stripped of its leaves, flowers and fruit; nothing is left but the branches, the trunk and the roots, which are always there. Similarly, brutes, ordinary men and men of talent are always plentiful in the world, whereas geniuses, saints and great Masters are much rarer. In winter, when the leaves, flowers and fruit of summer have all disappeared, we have only the memory of their colours, scents and flavours: all that beauty lingers on in our mind's eye. And the same is true of geniuses, saints and the Masters: for a long time after they have left this world men still speak of their deeds and of the joy they spread around them. On earth, conditions are not very conducive to love, wisdom, beauty and truth. Geniuses, saints and great Masters visit the earth spreading far and near their colours, scents and flavour, and then they leave again. On earth, the only things that are permanent are mediocrity and ugliness. But in Heaven, on the contrary, it is the leaves, flowers and fruit that are eternal; all the rest is transitory.

If you observe yourselves you will have to acknowledge that in you, too, it is the roots, trunk and branches that are stable, tough and enduring, that is, the instincts, passions and purely personal tendencies. From time to time you will find some leaves in your intelligence (luminous thoughts), flowers in your soul (warm feelings) and fruits (impersonal, disinterested actions). But, unfortunately, the springtime is all too brief and, once again, all its beauty disappears. Your inspirations, the subtle states of your higher consciousness, fade rapidly and you are left as you were before, with the same need to eat, drink, quarrel and use everything to your own advantage.

But let us go even further with this analysis and we shall find more of the extraordinary correspondences that exist in nature. If you look at the diagram you will notice that the roots are connected to the fruit at the top: the roots are the starting point and the fruit is the end point. Once the fruit is ripe the roots pause in their work. The fruit and the seeds within them are future roots from which a new stem will spring. The fact that some plants bear their fruit on the roots (tubers), is an indication of that connection between roots and fruit. Tubers are plants which have been incapable of developing on the spiritual level: they have stayed underground. You can also see that there is a connection between the trunk and the flowers, and between the branches and leaves. And it is the same in man: the physical body is linked to the spirit, the heart is linked to the soul and the intellect to the causal body. This explains why there is this connection between the great Masters and brutes, between ordinary men and saints and between men of talent and geniuses.

And now let's look at the diagram (figure 16) to see what it can tell us about music.

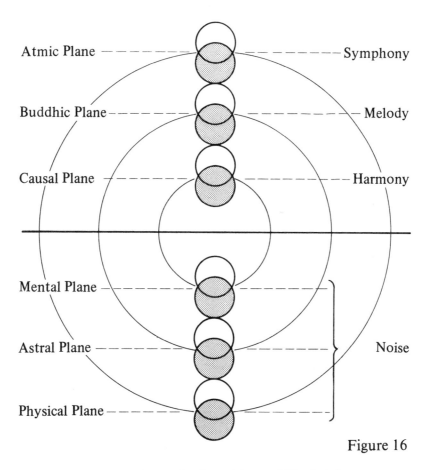

Figure 16

You all know what noise is and how difficult it is to put up with! Noise prevents concentration and fatigues and irritates us. Music and harmony, on the contrary, give us joy, inspiration and delight; they reveal higher worlds to us and put us in direct touch with them. Noise can be seen as the symbol of disharmony and it exists on the physical, astral and mental levels. On the higher levels, however, one enters immediately into the domain of music : harmony, melody and symphony. If you study music from the point of view of magic you will see that sound possesses great power and that musical vibrations produce varied and numerous forms. Harmonious sounds produce symmetrical forms whereas discordant sounds produce asymmetric forms. If you understood the magical power of sounds you would sing '*Aoum*' very differently from the way you sing it at present, for this song which is very ancient, produces splendid forms in the soul. If you were ready for it I would give you some exercises with which you could create harmonious forms in and around yourselves. When you play the chord C-E-G, for instance, you create a wonderful form : that chord is a world coming into being...

A true Initiate knows music and understands it ; he can use it to calm and heal people, and even to tame wild animals, for the vibrations of sound have real power.

If you knew what riches the Brotherhood possesses in its songs and melodies you would make the effort to sing well in order to benefit from them. It depends entirely on you. If you are well disposed anything is possible. If, before coming here, you prepare yourselves inwardly, you will see for yourselves what can be achieved in this hall. All around you are beings of a higher order who are trying to work with you ; if you are receptive they will sow good seed in you, and that which is already sown will sprout and grow strong. If you remain on your own the seeds within you cannot sprout : we need the help of those luminous beings of the invisible world who come into our souls in order for the seeds to start sprouting.

There was an article, recently, by a researcher who described the form of a flame when placed within the vibratory field of a musical instrument. If the flame is adjusted so that it is extremely sensitive and you play a very pure note on the violin, the flame assumes the shape of a head of wheat. But if you produce a discordant note the flame takes the form of a sprig of Rye-grass or tares.

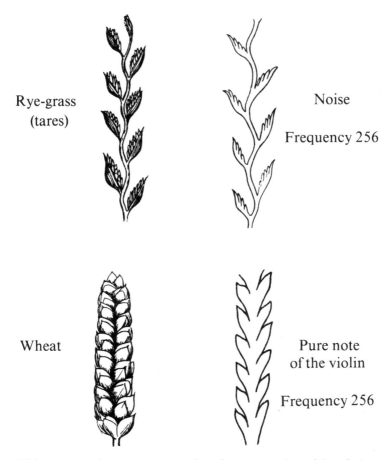

Rye-grass
(tares)

Noise

Frequency 256

Wheat

Pure note
of the violin

Frequency 256

This means that someone who always works with wisdom (eternal harmony), love (eternal melody) and truth (eternal symphony, that Music of the Spheres which only very few Masters have been able to hear), such a man will produce wheat, fruit and flowers and all that is most wonderful in life. Whereas the thoughts and feelings of evildoers produce only tares: thorns, wild beasts and poisonous plants. Wheat symbolizes the purest forms of food with which we should nourish not only our physical bodies but also our minds and hearts.

Rye-grass, as its name indicates,* makes one drunk and, of course, clouds the intelligence and upsets the balance of forces. All those who are drunk with pleasure, alcohol, wild behaviour or ephemeral glory nourish themselves with rye-grass or tares. Look carefully at the forms of the head of wheat and of the rye-grass and you will understand a world of truths. The rye-grass expresses all that is most unruly, chaotic and passionate, whereas wheat expresses all that is wise, balanced and harmonious.

It says in the parable: 'While men slept, his enemy came and sowed tares among the wheat'. But this is something that is happening all the time, all over the world: people are constantly emitting black thoughts and feelings which produce negative effects on the souls of those around them. Flowers and fruit, on the other hand, are formed by angels and archangels, by gods: their songs, their thoughts and feelings penetrate the atmosphere and give birth to all that is most beautiful and best and most spiritual on the earth. Just, good men also contribute to a richer harvest of fruit and wheat, whereas only weeds are produced by those who harbour sentiments of jealousy, hatred and revenge. If there were great numbers of good, pure human beings, the world would know abundance beyond words to describe. Unfortunately there are always more who spend their time sending out quantities of destructive thoughts and feelings into the world. Tares are everywhere: in philosophy, the sciences, education, literature, the arts.

Let me give you another example of what rye-grass is: who can lend me a coin? Now, watch as I put it into this envelope, which I then seal up in another envelope. I strike it

---

* Rye-grass, or Ray-grass as it used to be called, seems to derive its name from the same root as 'ivresse', meaning drunkenness in French. (Translator's note)

three times and, lo and behold, your coin has been reduced to dust! Isn't that extraordinary? Now, to console the person who lent me the coin, I shall now put it back together again. I put the powder into the two envelopes, I make a magic sign over it and there is your coin again! Now, unfortunately, that was just a trick and there is nothing to get excited about, but it just illustrates the fact that we meet people in the world who are always trying to dazzle us with their lies and their conjuring tricks, making glowing promises they never keep. Oh yes! A lot of people will offer you rye-grass to eat and try to persuade you that it is really wheat!

Now this is something you must realize; it is very important: a philosophy or teaching that does not fill you with the joy of strength, light and love, is nothing but weeds. True wheat nourishes you and makes you strong, it fills you with love, light and gladness.

Wheat is the symbol of perfection in the plant world. Look at its life-story: It is reaped by men, tied in bundles, threshed and sent to the mill to be ground into flour. Once it has been reduced to flour it is mixed with water, kneaded repeatedly and then put in the oven, where the fire cooks it. And just when it thinks its trials are over, human beings start chewing it. Many a mystery lies hidden in the life-story of a grain of wheat! And the evolution of man follows the same pattern, leading up to the moment when, like wheat, he will at last be fit to be offered as a holocaust for the salvation of mankind.

When you eat bread, the grain of wheat tells its story to your subconscious. It says, 'Be patient! God is good. He will be at your side to guide you through all your trials. Courage! I'm only a tiny grain of wheat but I'm there to help you, too. I can give you life, strength and joy. Follow my example; I'm very small and yet I feed the whole world and you, who are very big, you can't feed anybody but yourself without complaining and rebelling against it. Don't you think I was surrounded with weeds, myself? But I kept quiet about it, I put up with it all.'

There is a tradition that Venus brought us wheat and bees and that Earth, out of jealousy, created rye-grass and wasps!

Tolstoy tells a very lovely story based on a legend about a grain of wheat, and when I was Principal of a college in Bulgaria, I had the idea of making a play out of it and getting my pupils to act it. The legend tells of how, one day, a king picked up a seed, about the size of a hazelnut. He tried to find out where it had come from but failed. So he called on all the wise men at court, but none of them could tell him where it came from. However, the king heard that there was a very old man in his kingdom who would, perhaps, be able to tell him what he wanted to know, so he sent for him and the old man arrived, almost blind and walking with two crutches. After looking at the seed for a long time, the old man said, 'Your Majesty, I don't know where this enormous seed has come from, but if you will allow me, I shall call my father; perhaps he will remember having seen seeds like this before.' The father of the old man arrived, walking with the help of only one crutch and still hale and hearty. He was in a great rage, though, because his own father had thrashed him because he maintained he did not work hard enough. He was shown the seed, but he was no more able to tell where it came from than his son, so he suggested that he fetch his own father. After a while, therefore, the grandfather arrived, looking like a young man, strong, cheerful and robust. Snatching up the seed, he exclaimed in astonishment, 'Why, it's a grain of wheat such as used to grow when I was a child. In those days wheat had very big grains, but since men have taken to stealing and murdering, the grains of wheat have got smaller and smaller. And do you know why I am so strong and younger than my son or my grandson? It's because I still live according to the rules of honesty and goodness that prevailed in my youth'. The play was a great success!

Nowadays, the tendency is to try and uproot the weeds before the harvest with the result that the good wheat growing with it is uprooted too. This is the very worst method. The only effectual teaching is that which wheat offers, but the world will understand this only when all the wheat has been destroyed and it is crying out for bread. It is suffering that will teach men the meaning of the other method, the method of love.

It is not up to us to see that the wicked are destroyed. God alone can do justice. Our job is to be concerned only with good, to study and work for good. The more we contribute to the spiritual power of good, the more this power will limit the action and influence of evildoers. Higher forces can transform the wicked, but not we: we are far too weak. If we neglect to keep constantly in touch with the spirit of God we shall be powerless against evil, in fact we shall be contributing to its power, to the point of letting it destroy us.

One day everything will be ready for the harvest. When that day comes all the evil in the world will be absorbed and soaked up by the earth. My dear brothers and sisters, you have no notion of all the work that is going on on the spiritual level. Sublime entities have been sent to restore order on earth and, as they descend, the spirits of darkness flee before them and take refuge in animals and also in men. This is why the ignorant and the wicked are visited by these spirits of darkness who encourage and reinforce them in their lawless, anarchical ways. And this will go on until all evil has been exterminated. It is the earth that has been designated to absorb and swallow up evil, as St. John explains in Revelation, saying that the Dragon (evil) will be cast down and shut up under the earth by the Archangel Mikhaël. If there is so much crime in the world today it is because people are receptive to these entities fleeing before the angels of light. And it is for this reason, also, that we must not eat animal flesh, for they, too, are being occupied by evil entities.

Anyone who thinks he can get rid of a criminal by executing him is making a great mistake : once dead on the physical plane, he is free to move onto the astral and lower mental planes where he can do even more damage. In his determination to revenge himself he can worm his way into people's minds and drive them to commit crimes so as to accomplish his evil designs through them. In fact he has more possibilities for action open to him than before his death, since he is no longer limited to one physical body : he can use many different people. When a liquid with a nauseating smell is in a sealed bottle, the smell cannot spread, but if you open the bottle the smell instantly pervades the whole house. In the same way, as long as a criminal is alive he is confined to his own body, but once he dies he is liberated, he can pervade the atmosphere and enter a great many human minds in order to influence them. Criminals should not be executed because of the consequences this entails on the invisible plane. It is up to us to organize things in such a way that there will be no more malefactors. An education and a way of life that are not founded on spiritual laws are like swamps, and a swamp breeds only mosquitos! The number of malefactors in the world will never diminish if mankind does not decide to found society on the principles which already exist in nature.

Criminals should not be executed, but nor should they be set free : they should be put to work and kept busy. Even the very worst criminals can be transformed by the laws of love, wisdom and truth. If we do not manage to transform them it is because we do not have enough love, wisdom or truth, ourselves. Look at Pestalozzi : he was neither an Initiate nor a great Master, so how did he discover the true educational method? He was one of the greatest educators of all times : he took in juvenile delinquents and transformed them with the power of his love. He discovered the true laws of education because he loved these children and wanted to transform them and for that he was willing to sacrifice a great deal. No one can change people if he is not prepared to make sacrifices. Nowadays, everyone tries to do only what is easy and agreeable and hopes to get wonderful results without having to make an effort. Unfortunately this attitude does not correspond to any natural law: on the contrary, Nature declares, 'When one gives only a little, one learns only a little and one receives only a little'. There is no other law: the more one gives one's heart, mind and will to the divine cause, the more wisdom, love and truth one receives. The more completely one consecrates oneself to the world above, the more joy, freedom, riches and blessings does one receive. There! That is something solid.

I repeat: 'The day will come, and it is already near, when evil will be expelled from this earth, the Archangel Mikhaël will come and lay hold of the dragon and bind him in the bottomless pit for a thousand years. That is the time of the harvest.' All the evil in us is part of the cosmic evil and when this (in the form of the dragon) is cast into the bottomless pit, it will take with it all the evil which is in us. It is then that there will be much weeping and gnashing of teeth for this purification will be accomplished with great heat and great suffering. The invisible world will send fire to purify the earth and it is then that the tares within us will be separated from the wheat. At the moment, the earth is already under the fire and he who has allowed a lot of tares to grow within him will suffer terribly, for the fire that must come will penetrate everything. But he who has much wheat will rejoice; he will be like a lamp and his flame will become brighter and brighter, for the fire from heaven that will consume the tares, will only illuminate the Sons of God's Kingdom.

Paris, May 21, 1938

9

Spiritual Alchemy

First of all I would like to read you these two passages, from the Book of Exodus and from the Gospel of St. John.

'And the Lord spake unto Moses and unto Aaron, saying, When Pharaoh shall speak unto you, saying, Shew a miracle for you: then thou shalt say unto Aaron, Take thy rod, and cast it before Pharaoh, and it shall become a serpent. And Moses and Aaron went in unto Pharaoh, and they did so as the Lord had commanded: and Aaron cast down his rod before Pharaoh, and before his servants, and it became a serpent. Then Pharaoh also called the wise men and the sorcerers: now the magicians of Egypt, they also did in like manner with their enchantments. For they cast down every man his rod, and they became serpents: but Aaron's rod swallowed up their rods. And he hardened Pharaoh's heart, that he hearkened not unto them; as the Lord had said...

And the Lord spake unto Moses, Say unto Aaron, Take thy rod, and stretch out thine hand upon the waters of Egypt, upon their streams, upon their rivers, and upon their ponds, and upon all their pools of water, that they may become blood; and that there may be blood throughout all the land of Egypt, both in vessels of wood, and in vessels of stone. And Moses and Aaron did so, as the Lord commanded; and he lifted up the rod, and smote the waters that were in the river, in the sight of Pharaoh, and in the sight of his servants; and all the waters that were in the river were turned to blood. And the fish that was in the river died; and the river stank, and the Egyptians could not drink of the waters of the river; and there was blood throughout all the land of Egypt.'

Exodus 7 : 8-13, 19-21

'And the third day there was a marriage in Cana of Galilee; and the mother of Jesus was there: And both Jesus was called, and his disciples, to the marriage. And when they wanted wine, the mother of Jesus saith unto him, They have no wine. Jesus saith unto her, Woman, what have I to do with thee? mine hour is not yet come. His mother saith unto the servants, Whatsoever he saith unto you, do it.

And there were set there six water-pots of stone, after the manner of the purifying of the Jews, containing two or three firkins apiece.

Jesus saith unto them, Fill the water-pots with water, And they filled them up to the brim. And he saith unto them, Draw out now and bear unto the governor of the feast. And they bare it. When the ruler of the feast had tasted the water that was made wine, and knew not whence it was: (but the servants which drew the water knew;) the governor of the feast called the bridegroom, and saith unto him, Every man at the beginning doth set forth good wine; and when men have well drunk, then that which is worse: but thou hast kept the good wine until now.

This beginning of miracles did Jesus in Cana of Galilee, and manifested forth his glory: and his disciples believed on him.'

John 2 : 1-11

Yesterday I talked to you at length about the parable of the wheat and the tares, explaining that they were symbols of good and evil which are so closely bound up together in the world that if we try to destroy the tares we run the risk of uprooting the wheat along with the weeds. They have to continue to grow side by side, therefore, until harvest time.

And today I want to discuss these same symbols, but as they apply to man himself.

Tares, or weeds, are the symbol of our lower nature. Now, in fact, our lower nature is not evil: it does the work it has been created for and we cannot blame it. However the conditions that prevail within that lower nature are the perfect setting for the germination and growth of the harmful seeds sown in it by the enemy of humanity, the spirit of evil. Our lower nature harbours this destructive element which gnaws away at it like a cancer, draining it of its vital forces, so that, in the end, the human spirit is forced to abandon it in order to free itself. The harvest time spoken of in the Gospels comes, for each individual human being, at the moment of his death, but it will also come one day for humanity as a whole.

Religious and moral leaders are making a mistake when they advise people to try to uproot evil and vice in themselves; this method has never produced good results. The branches of a tree are linked to the roots and, if you cut off the roots the branches wither and die, and it is exactly the same with us: our higher states are linked to the existence of our roots. If we allow certain cells of our body complete freedom to manifest themselves we shall be led into serious irregularities, but that does not mean that in order to avoid being led astray we have to tear those cells out of our bodies. On the contrary, we have to draw strength from them, for the organs located below the diaphragm are like great factories producing the materials and energy required for the activities of the spirit. A lot of pious people think that sexual energy is evil and in order to avoid becoming its slave, they think we should become eunuchs! The only trouble is that those who follow this advice then become incapable of achieving anything worthwhile in life; they understand nothing in science, philosophy or the arts because they are deprived of all inspiration*.

Inspiration, like the joy we experience when we contemplate beauty, springs from the sexual energies which are not, as we have so often been told, satanic forces. The evil in man has been represented as a serpent, but the serpent is harmful only to the ignorant or the wicked and to those who refuse to do God's will. For Initiates it is a perfect servant. The Caballah teaches that the Spirit of Impurity assumed the form of a serpent when he tempted Adam and Eve. The name of that Spirit is Samaël. When our first parents were still in the Garden of Eden they studied the properties of the elements (symbolized by the different trees in the Garden), but they were incapable of neutralizing or of resisting the influence of the poison this evil spirit implanted, first of all, in Eve.

In our daily lives we are all exposed to attack by all kinds of poisons, and some people react positively while others fall ill. Take the example of stings or bites from insects: some people are really quite ill from nothing more than a mosquito or flea bite, or the sting of a wasp, whereas others hardly even feel it: they are invulnerable, like the hedgehog which is not even affected by a snakebite. So why are some people capable of reacting and defending themselves by counteracting harmful substances and others are not? If you asked fleas or bedbugs their opinion, they would say that their scientific research has led them to the conclusion that people who live in impurity have delicious blood whereas the blood of those who are pure tastes horrible!

And then, too, why do some people actually fall ill if someone says something slightly negative about them whereas

* See 'Good and Evil' and 'How to Measure Up to the Dragon' in *Complete Works*, vol. 5; 'Love and Sexuality' in vol. 7 and 'Materialism, Idealism and Sexuality' in vol. 15.

others do not even notice the venom in a deliberate insult or offensive remark?

The verses from Exodus that I read to you a few moments ago, which tell of how Aaron's rod was changed, first of all, into a serpent and then into a magic wand, conceal secrets that belong to the highest degrees of initiation. The serpent has always been seen to symbolize both the spirit of evil and wisdom. And the Caduceus of Hermes, which you all know, is a wand with two intertwined serpents.

For an Initiate, the first serpent represents sexual energy, the source of evil, and the second symbolizes the transformation and sublimation of this sexual energy into another, very powerful force: wisdom and clairvoyance. It is for this reason that the ancient Pharaohs of Egypt were often represented with a tiny serpent growing out from between their eyes. This means that they had transmuted their sexual energy by raising it to the level of the brain. And this transmuted force enabled the Initiates to glimpse the subtle realities of the supraterrestrial regions. In some of the religions of Antiquity serpents were venerated and used as oracles: this was the case at Delphi, for example, where the Pythia was believed to pronounce her oracles under the inspiration of the Python. There is also the symbol of the serpent coiled in a spiral or that of a serpent swallowing its own tail : both of them come from extremely ancient traditions. Wise men who know the laws and know how to transform that force lying dormant in each one of us, become serpents, that is to say, prudent, reasoning beings. In India, sages are also called 'nagi', which means serpents, to signify that the forces of evil can become beneficial forces if man knows how to transform them. The serpent within us is in the backbone. The serpent power, Kundalini, is coiled up asleep at the base of the spine and, for the Initiate who is capable of awakening it, it can perform miracles.

Poison is condensed, extremely powerful matter. Our first parents were forbidden to eat the fruit of the Tree of the Knowledge of Good and Evil because it contained elements which they were not yet ready to assimilate ; they had to wait. In a way the Garden of Eden was an alchemist's laboratory and Adam and Eve were alchemists who wanted to explore all the great secrets of nature. But they were too curious and went too fast; like so many 'sorcerer's apprentices' which abound in the history of occult science, they were not ready for the experiments they undertook. Perhaps you know Bulwer Lytton's novel, 'Zanoni', for instance. One night, Glyndon, Mejnour's pupil, decides to defy his Master's orders and goes into the secret closet where he keeps a flask of the Elixir of Everlasting Life. Opening the flask he breathes in its fragrance and bathes his temples with the liquid and begins to experience the most extraordinary sensations. But after only a few seconds of bliss, he finds himself face to face with a terrifying monster: the Guardian of the Threshhold and, unable to endure this horrifying sight, he faints. Later, constantly pursued by this monster, he would have gone out of his mind if Zanoni had not come to his rescue. And this is how so many occultists fall prey to hostile entities: they dash headlong at the great mysteries of nature, supposedly in order to develop their clairvoyance or their magical powers, without having prepared themselves by years of meditation, prayer and fasting.

All things in creation have been prepared by God for His children. All that He has created is good; but it is good for us only at the pre-ordained moment, when we are ready. Do you eat sour, unripe grapes? Do you give an infant the same things to eat as you give an adult?

God, therefore, had forbidden Adam and Eve to eat the fruit of the Tree of the Knowledge of Good and Evil. And Eve, who was more inquisitive than Adam, looked at them longingly, although she did not dare touch them, for she was aware of her ignorance. But then the serpent in her spine awoke, for it was very hot. As you know, in hot weather snakes wake up and become extremely agile and rapid; if you want to render them harmless, you have to put them in the cold. However, on that particular day, it was very hot in the Garden of Eden (this is all symbolic, of course), and the serpent coiled up in Eve's backbone awoke and whispered in her ear, 'Try it! Just take a little bite to taste the fruit. What are you afraid of? If you eat it you will become like God Himself. That's why He's forbidden you to eat it'. It is true that Eve will, one day, become like God because of that fruit, but only after billions of years of suffering and vicissitudes of every kind; only after innumerable incarnations. So Eve ate the forbidden fruit and gave some to Adam, too. But they were unable to assimilate it. God had told them that if they ate that fruit they would die, and die they did, in the sense that they underwent a change of consciousness. Before that they had been free, happy, weightless and luminous, but now they died to that higher state; they died to joy and to the light of Heaven and they came alive to the sufferings of the earth.

You will have understood, of course, that the serpent spoken of in Genesis is also a symbol; the symbol of the sexual

energy in man which was awakened and to which man suc-
cumbed. The serpent is roused when it is hot and sleeps when
it is cold. In every form of passion there is heat, a heat that
destroys and consumes us inwardly. In the torrid forests of the
equator lurk wild animals and beasts of prey and he who
spends a lot of his time at the equator (stomach and sex) has
to contend with his passions (wild beasts), which begin to gain
the upper hand. If the fire with which you attempt to warm
another is the fire of passion, you will arouse the wild beasts
in him. You must always try to avoid the heat of the passions; this is why Initiates do not allow their disciples to remain in the heat, they put them in the cold. Let me give you
an example: suppose you enjoy great wealth and fame; figu-
ratively you are living in a warm climate with an abundance
of everything. These are the ideal conditions for the serpent to
become active, and if you are unable to dominate the situation, you will begin to indulge yourselves in all kinds of pleasures and amusements and, gradually, you will sink lower and
lower to the regions of Hell. This is why it is far better for
those who are still weak not to have too great an abundance of
worldly goods so as to be sure of maintaining control of the
serpents within.

Heat and cold are two occult methods used by Initiates. In
the cold there is neither putrefaction nor wild beasts. But I am
not talking about physical cold: I am talking about that place
where death no longer exists, where there is no more sickness.
All the heavenly forces that are distributed throughout the
earth come to us from the North Pole which is inhabited by
the highest and purest of immortal beings: the Gods. The au-
rora borealis is an accidental manifestation of the auras of
those who live at the Pole. You may doubt my words but, one
day, science will discover the truth of these secrets. From the
spiritual point of view the North Pole is the most exalted spot
on this earth.

A great many people fear sexual energy, but it is this that supplies energy to all the cells of the body. Of course, it needs to be handled with great care, for it is a raw, untamed force which has to be transformed in the cells and distributed by the spirit to the whole being, in the form of vitality in the physical body, love and joy in the heart and light and wisdom in the mind. Sexual energy is a great turbulent river but Initiates place watermills in all the strategic spots in order to harness its power. They do not let it torment them or drive them into tragic situations; they do not allow it to flood their towns and villages; they build factories and irrigation ditches and they reap the fruits produced in them by this power they have so wisely channeled and portioned out. The more one uses one's reason in handling one's sexual energy, the richer one becomes in spiritual things. Sexual force, once mastered, is like a great river that has been led off into canals and ditches to irrigate the land. You know what wealth and power was the lot of ancient Egypt because of the Nile.

The more one draws on one's sexual energy wisely, the better one is able to understand the Kingdom of God, the Angels and Archangels and all that is beautiful in life. All Initiates are agreed on this score: they even say that if a man wastes his sexual energy or fails to control it, it will serve to feed the ghosts of the astral world. It is men, therefore, who are responsible for strengthening those inferior entities who then harry and torment them mercilessly, seeking to weaken and impoverish them: but they are the last to realize that it is they themselves who have nourished and encouraged their enemies to their cost. But I cannot say very much about this subject: the question is a delicate one and each individual has to find his own solutions. All I can do is give you a few explanations and examples: then it will be up to you to find what suits you. The examples I use are mostly from the plant world, for the laws involved are always obvious. Plants are marvellous alchemists: if you want to learn how to work with matter, you should study plants.

The methods I reveal to you are of very considerable value for your own lives. If you understand me correctly, you will possess Aaron's magic wand which will become a serpent and swallow up all the other serpents so that you will be invulnerable. So, once again, today, I shall open the great book of Nature before you, for a few brief moments, and read you a page. Make the most of it!

Have you ever noticed how tense you become when you are struggling against yourself, and how many difficulties you encounter? There is a terrible war going on within you and you are tossed in all directions, in a constant state of contradiction. You are convinced that everything in your lower nature is necessarily your enemy and you are determined to kill it. But this enemy is very powerful (for centuries you have been waging war against it and it has become stronger and stronger) and the threat it represents increases day by day. Take the example of love: people shut themselves up in convents to escape from it with the result that they think about it more and more every day. And even if you flee into the desert where your only companions are the rocks and stones, it is still useless. You can read certain pious books and eat special food... all to no avail. All this means is that our philosophy is based on false premises. As long as one sees the force of love as an enemy to be destroyed one will never get any lasting results. We may cut off one of the Hydra's heads but in no time at all it will have grown a new one, for they all grow again. Our methods are ineffectual because we cling stubbornly to the notion that the enemy is within us. It is true that we have enemies within us, but they are enemies only because we are not properly informed, nor are we good, enlightened or patient. The only thing that is really wrong is that we are very poor alchemists, incapable of transforming anything.

That which is harmful for ordinary men is wonderfully useful for Initiates. You say that suffering is terrible and hateful, but Initiates say that it is the raw material from which they draw the elements they need to evolve and grow stronger. The sufferings you complain about are the pigments which are indispensable to the painter. A man who has not had to endure a certain amount of suffering will never find the colours he needs to create a fine work of art.

The sun sends light and life on to the earth, and men, animals and plants absorb it. We suck in life and discard our waste matter, our sins, which the sun transforms and sends back to us in the form of life. This ceaseless circulation between the earth and the sun exists also between ordinary men and the Initiates. Initiates gather up the raw, unrefined materials, transform them and send them to us in the form of all kinds of treasures. If we want to be intelligent we must stop thinking about all the weaknesses and faults we see in others and start working to transform them. When we work to transform the weakness and wickedness of those around us we are working for the Kingdom of God and the Initiates will accept us as disciples. They will say, 'Come with us. You are ready to help us and we need people to collaborate in our work'.

Some of you may react to all this: 'Overcome difficulties, transform the weaknesses and wickedness of others... that's all very fine, but it's not for us! We are no alchemists'. But then, I ask you, how did the pearl oyster solve its problem? When a grain of sand gets into an oyster's shell it cannot push it out: it has neither hands, nor feet, nor tentacles. So it thinks hard and meditates on the problem and finds an answer which makes of it a great alchemist: it begins to secrete a special substance in which it wraps the grain of sand, thus turning it into a pearl. You know how much everyone appreciates pearls, and yet they are only grains of sand wrapped up! And if we, human beings, are incapable of transforming the obstacles and difficulties of life, it must mean that we are less intelligent than an oyster! Every enemy and every difficulty we meet with in life can be transformed into a pearl. This is why the Initiates own a great many pearls. If we were to ask them how they became so rich and why they distribute so many pearls to all their friends, they would tell us that it is because they understood the law that enables one to transform enemies into friends and all the difficult things in life into pearls of great price. Study the oyster's methods. As human beings you are privileged: you have arms and hands, a mouth, eyes, ears, a brain, etc. How is it that you have still not discovered how to make a pearl?

The Pharisees who were always anxious to be admitted into the company of the rich and important members of society, who jockeyed for first place in their assemblies and ceremonies and who despised the poor, proved that they did not understand the methods of true alchemy. They could not understand why Jesus sought the company of ignorant, sinful, unlettered people. Mary Magdalen was condemned by everybody except Jesus who gave her a warm, loving welcome. But Jesus knew the law of transmutation and thanks to him she became that pearl of great price that people talk about, even now.

Yesterday we studied the functions of the different parts of a tree: roots, trunk, branches, leaves, flowers and fruit, and we saw how each corresponds to a certain type of individual. Today we shall study another phenomenon: the sap and how it rises in the stem of a plant.

Raw sap is the water and dissolved mineral nutrients drawn from the soil by the roots of a tree. Absorbed by the fine root hairs, the sap flows through the outer layers of the root to the main vessel system through which it rises to the trunk and leaves.

Three different mechanisms are involved in this work:

Osmosis – Capillary action – Transpiration

– By osmosis, soil water with a low concentration of mineral salts is drawn through the membranes of root hairs into the cells which contain a higher concentration of salts.

– By capillary action, liquids are drawn up to the leaves, through the extremely fine conduits of vegetable tissue.

– Transpiration is the phenomenon by which the leaves shed excess water from the sap they receive. The upward flow of sap, therefore, increases due to the suction exerted by the leaves.

In the functioning of the human body, the same mechanisms – osmosis, capillary action and transpiration – can be found. Osmosis and capillary action are particularly important in the mechanisms of circulation of the blood, digestion and respiration. But transpiration is the function that seems to be the least understood, and as it is very important, I propose to talk about it today.

You know that, except for the fact that it is far less concentrated, sweat has the same chemical composition as urine. The skin, by eliminating sweat through its pores, carries out the same function, therefore, as the kidneys. Transpiration, or perspiration as we call it when we are speaking of the human body, is a means by which man cleanses and purifies himself. There are several different ways to induce perspiration but I can recommend one very simple method: drink hot water. Boil the water and drink it as hot as possible. By osmosis, the hot water enters all the different tracts and conduits of the body, dilating them and, by capillary action rises to the surface of the skin where it is transpired through the pores. When you perspire like this you feel refreshed, purified, strengthened. Perspiration is vital for the health of the body. If you have caught cold, for instance, and you are starting to run a temperature, you can cure yourself by inducing perspiration with several cups of very hot water which will help you get rid of your toxins.

But physical transpiration is not enough. The soul and spirit also need to 'transpire'. And love is the hot water that induces transpiration in the soul: wisdom, the divine water, induces transpiration in the spirit. You realize, of course, that you must understand the word 'transpiration' in a very broad sense. It symbolizes that perfect relationship of exchange between the microcosmos (man) and the macrocosmos (the universe). On the physical level, exchanges take place through the skin: the skin rids the body of wastes and receives an input of energy. But on the higher, subtler levels, these exchanges take place through the aura, our spiritual skin. So, when I say that, like our physical bodies, our souls and spirits must perspire, also, I am simply saying that exchanges on the subtler levels are equally vital.

In a previous lecture* I explained the symbolic significance of the three leaf pigments (chlorophyll, carotin and xanthophyll) by means of which a plant absorbs light and uses it to produce glucose. Chlorophyll is green, carotin is orange-yellow and xanthophyll is yellow. If we take their complementary colours, red, blue and violet, we find we have the triangle representing the three principles of will, mind and heart which correspond, in our bodies, to the three organs: brain, heart (and lungs) and stomach which, in turn, correspond to the three bodily functions of nutrition, respiration and reflection.

When we eat, our stomach, which uses green, attracts the red rays. Red symbolizes life and energy. When we eat correctly our vital forces are strengthened: red and green are united.

* See 'Love Concealed in the Mouth', *Complete Works,* vol. 1

Chlorophyll *green*	Red rays
Carotin *orange*	Blue rays
Xanthophyll *yellow*	Violet rays

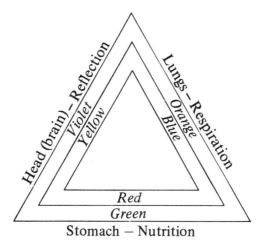

Figure 17

To recapitulate, therefore :

Chlorophyll – stomach – nutrition
Carotin – heart and lungs – respiration
Xanthophyll – brain – reflection

When we breathe, our lungs, which use orange, attract the blue rays. Blue stands for peace and harmony. If he breathes harmoniously, rythmically, man feels peace and calm seeping into his whole being : orange and blue have come together.

When we meditate, our brain, which uses yellow, attracts the violet rays, and violet is the colour of the highest forms of spirituality. Through meditation man unites himself with the Divinity; yellow is united to violet.

And now, if you have understood me correctly, you have all you need to become proficient alchemists and to transform the raw sap (that is, thoughts which are without light, feelings which are without warmth and chaotic, inharmonious actions) within you. If you put this raw sap through the three processes of nutrition, respiration and reflection, it will be transformed into the elaborated, sweet sap that nourishes the whole body. But if these three functions are to be perfectly accomplished there is a different rule to be observed for each one.

For digestion to be perfect it has to remain within the limits of life.

For respiration to be perfect it has to remain within the limits of love.

For reflection to be perfect it has to remain within the limits of wisdom.

So, from what we have just said, we can conclude that:

1. Digestion is the function by which we act on raw materials on the physical level;

2. Respiration is the function by which we act on raw materials on the spiritual level, and

3. Meditation is the function by which we act on raw materials on the divine level.

In these three fundamental processes of human life, Nature has hidden the most potent means available to man for the transformation of his own life. Unfortunately, men always try to keep themselves in good physical and moral shape by methods other than those indicated by Nature; but they try in vain, for neither pills nor potions nor the the prick of the needle does any good. The trouble is that men find Nature's methods difficult so they cheat, trying to find ways of improving their situation that will make no demands on them. Sometimes, when he is on his deathbed, a man will realize he is completely bankrupt and say, at last, that he has understood. But has he really? In any event, by then it is too late; it is already time for him to leave this earth. People wait until they are old and then try to bluff their way into Paradise by lighting a few votive candles in church! When young they waste all their substance on senseless follies; when old and decrepit they begin to think about God and imagine all He asks of them is their last minute repentance and they will be given a seat at His right hand! No, you must understand that the only means of salvation is the sincere desire to learn and to work at one's own perfection in order to do God's will.

While they are on this earth men spend their whole lives transforming matter: everything they eat is converted into blood, nerves and flesh, bones, teeth, nails and hair. Man is already an alchemist but he does not know it.

In alchemical texts it says that silver has to be transmuted into gold. Hidden behind these two symbols, silver and gold, the moon and the sun, lie the most profound secrets. The whole of alchemical science consists in the art of turning fire into air, air into water and water into earth. Alchemists used many different ways to express the same truth. When Aaron changes the waters of the Nile into blood or when Jesus changes the water into wine at the Marriage Feast of Cana, it is still the same truth expressed in different ways. Water is green and green must be transformed into red: blood and wine. You perform this transmutation every single day without even realizing it. To change silver to gold, the moon into the sun or green into red, is to change what is ephemeral, transitory and illusory into something solid, incorruptible and precious. If you want to succeed in this you must first study the laws of transmutation. You must earn the privilege of possessing the magic wand (the Caduceus of Hermes, Aaron's rod) and be capable of consciously controlling the two serpents, the two currents: the currents of electric and magnetic energy, of attraction and repulsion, love and hate. When one knows how to control and orient these two currents one can transform everything. In the language of alchemy, when one achieves the red, it means that one has the King, the Philosopher's Stone which is scarlet.

I cannot give you any more details about this question: it would be too long. I have given you what may seem to be scattered fragments and it is up to you, now, to relate them to each other and, in your meditations, to put them all in their proper place. Meditate, too on these symbols: on the physical level, red is the colour of woman and white is the colour of man. But on the spiritual level, it is white that is the colour of woman and red the colour of man. And now he who understands, let him study this question more deeply.

Aaron's rod became a serpent and swallowed up the serpents of all the other magicians. Like Aaron, the disciple who wants to become an Initiate must change his magic wand (his will) into a serpent, that is, into a mobile, subtle, living force. And that force must be potent enough to swallow up all venom of all the most hostile thoughts and feelings directed towards him by both visible and invisible enemies. On this condition only will he be recognized as a true Initiate, a true alchemist.

Paris, May 22, 1938

10

Spiritual Galvanoplasty

Today I shall read you a short passage from the Gospel of St. Matthew:

'Verily I say unto you, Whatsoever ye shall bind on earth shall be bound in Heaven: and whatsoever ye shall loose on earth shall be loosed in Heaven.

Again I say unto you, That if two of you agree on earth as touching any thing that they shall ask, it shall be done for them of my Father which is in Heaven. For where two or three are gathered together in my name, there am I in the midst of them.'

Matthew 18 : 18-20

Everyone has read these words, but without really understanding the underlying significance of this phrase: 'Whatsoever ye shall loose on earth shall be loosed in Heaven'. Why this correspondence between the earth and Heaven? Because Heaven and earth always represent the two active principles in the world: the masculine and feminine principles, the positive and negative poles, present in every phenomenon of nature and life. Between the two poles there is a constant flow of exchange.

See how it is in a human family: you have the father, the masculine principle and the mother, the feminine principle and between them, the child. The child is the link between the father and the mother. Within the human being, the masculine principle, the father, is the intellect; the feminine principle, the mother, is the heart, and the child is the action. All our acts are a consequence of our thoughts and feelings. When both our thoughts and our feelings are good, then our acts, which are the fruit of the wisdom of our intellects and the love in our hearts, will also be good and constructive. Man's strength is the result of the proper union of wisdom and love.

Action is always the child of the heart and the mind. One sometimes meets people who are very active, but whose hearts and intellects are not very well developed: that does not change the fact that their actions are the children of their hearts and minds... of their absence of heart and mind! Whether we act thoughtfully and with feeling or in a mental and emotional daze, we are still giving birth to an activity born of the intellect and the heart. What the child will be like, of course, depends entirely on the degree of evolution and culture of its parents. Acts are intelligent or stupid, good or bad, according to the state of our hearts and minds. So, there is always a father and a mother: a heaven and an earth.

Suppose you plant a seed in the ground: when you do that you are binding something on earth, for the seed will germinate, but you are also binding something in heaven. How? When you bury a seed in the soil there is immediately a link between the earth and all the stars in the heavens; the sun sends its light and heat to the seed which begins to grow. All you have done is put a seed or kernel in the ground, but in doing so you have set something in motion in heaven. And a similar process takes place within man himself. For instance, we bind something 'on earth' when we sow a seed (food) in the ground (our stomach); instantly, heaven (our brain) sends out currents to act on the food we have absorbed, transforming it into energy, emotions and thoughts. As soon as we put some food in our stomach, forces converge on it from all the other parts of the body, setting up a flow of exchange.

Binding and loosing: the two operations can be found in every area of existence. In analysis and synthesis, for example: when you synthesize something you are binding and when you analyze something you are loosing. In man it is the heart which binds and the intellect which looses. The heart synthesizes: it unites, assembles, gathers and creates bonds with the things it loves and, unfortunately, it often creates very unwise bonds... The intellect, on the contrary, analyzes, separates, destroys. In our day, when the intellect takes priority, it is in the process of destroying everything. It is time to restore the heart to its proper place, because it is the heart that vivifies, and creates unity, that brings things to life with its warmth and tenderness. When the heart has room to manifest itself in a family, the father and mother become more united, closer, more loving. But as soon as the intellect gets the upper hand, then the discussions and arguments begin and they end up by separating. Don't conclude, from this, that you should do away with your intellect: no, but the intellect must work in conjunction with the heart. In other words, when it needs to free itself, it will analyze and loosen certain things but without destroying them.

Just to make the respective functions of the heart and the intellect clearer to you and show you how they should work together, let me illustrate this with a story. One day, two men were brought up before the magistrate, accused of stealing apples by reaching over the wall surrounding the orchard. The people in the courtroom looked at them in amazement, for one of them had no legs and the other one was blind. The former said: 'Your Honour, as you can see, I haven't any

legs. How could I possibly climb up and reach over the wall
to get the apples?' And the other man said: 'Your Honour, I
haven't any eyes. I couldn't even see that there were some apples to steal!' The bench was about to throw out the case,
persuaded that they must be innocent, when one of the magistrates, more clearsighted than the others, said: 'Just a minute! Separately, of course, they couldn't have stolen the apples. But if the legless man was hoisted onto the shoulders of
the blind man... well, there you have a whole man! Together
they stole the apples'. What do these two thieves represent?
The heart and the intellect. The blind one is the heart. Everyone knows that the heart is blind but it can walk... in fact it
can gallop! All our strength, all our desires, are located in the
heart and it can take us wherever we want to go. The one who
has eyes to see and observe with is the intellect. But the intellect cannot walk, it needs help; the blind man has to carry
him on his shoulders. When heart and intellect are as one
they can do wonders: miracles or crimes.

The attributes of heart and mind can be found in every
area: physics, mathematics, botany, psychology, in fact they
manifest themselves in so many ways it would be impossible
to interpret them all. Inversely, every natural phenomenon
corresponds to a phenomenon in our own life, in our
thoughts and feelings. This evening I want to study the phenomenon of galvanoplasty or electroplating. On the physical
level everyone knows what this is, but they never stop to interpret it and see how it corresponds to something in us.

First of all, let me describe the physical phenomenon of
galvanoplasty.

Two electrodes are introduced into a bath containing a solution of metallic salts: gold, silver, copper, etc. The anode is
a sheet of the same metal as that in the solution and the cathode is a gutta-percha mould coated with graphite and
stamped with a design for a coin or medal, etc. The two elec-

trodes are wired to the two poles of a battery. Gradually, the metal in the solution coats the cathode and, at the same time, the anode decomposes thus providing a constant supply of metal into the solution. Little by little, as the cathode becomes more thickly coated with metal, you obtain the desired result : a medal stamped with the chosen design.

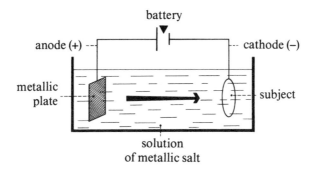

Figure 18

Now, if you look for corresponding phenomena on the spiritual level, you will see that electroplating exists throughout nature. The planet earth, for instance, represents the negative pole (cathode, woman), and the heavens (the sun and stars) represent the positive pole (anode, masculine principle). There is a ceaseless flow and interchange of currents between the earth and the sun (or any other star), because they are both immersed in a cosmic solution : the ether or universal fluid in which all the heavenly bodies are plunged. The battery, of course, is God, and all poles are connected to Him. And now, if we attach a mould of some kind, a seed for instance, to the cathode, it is immersed in the cosmic solution and the current flowing through the solution from God produces the same effects as in electroplating: particles of the material in the solution begin to build up on the seed while the sun or other star renews and regenerates the solution as the seedling grows up around the mould. Every seed planted in the soil, therefore, draws the elements it needs, according to its specific characteristics, from the surrounding ether and welds them to itself as it grows and develops.

In relation to the earth, each planet represents the positive pole, a particular anode. According to the type of mould attached to the cathode, one or other of these anodes will become active and supply the material with which the mould is to be coated. The earth is the cathode which becomes coated with the particles of metal salts dissolved in the universal solution. According to Initiatic Science, the Sun is the primordial gold and the source of all the gold found in nature: its rays condense in the ground in the form of gold dust. Similarly, each planet represents a particular metal: Saturn, lead; the Moon, silver; Jupiter, tin; Venus, copper; Mercury, quicksilver, and Mars, iron.

The phenomena of galvanoplasty can be seen at work in a pregnant woman and this is what I want to talk to you about today. A pregnant woman carries within her the seed, the electrodes and the solution. The seed is the living sperm implanted in her womb (the cathode) by the father. This seed is an image, and it may be that of a drunkard, a criminal or an ordinary, unexceptional human being; equally it may be the image of a saint or a genius. As soon as a woman is pregnant a current begins to flow between her brain (the anode) and the seed. The brain is connected to the battery (the stars, God) and receives energy from it, and this energy flows from the brain to the embryo. The solution is the mother's blood, in which both anode and cathode (the brain and the uterus) are immersed, for our blood bathes all our organs and cells and all the physical elements exist in solution in the blood, including gold, silver, copper, etc. The anode, therefore, supplies the precious metal contained in the mother's thoughts which regenerates the blood. The seed implanted in a woman's womb may be of very exceptional quality but if she has thoughts of lead in her mind (symbolically speaking) she need not be surprised if, later on, her child turns out to be a miserable, unhealthy weakling. You know that if you slice a lump of lead, the newly exposed surface is bright and shiny for a few minutes, then it becomes dull again. Similarly, a child that has been fed in the womb with leaden thoughts, will be withdrawn, unhappy and pessimistic. Even if he can sometimes be shaken out of his depression it is never for long, in no time at all he falls back into despondency or illness. And this is because the particles of matter in the mother's blood, and which corresponded to her own negative thoughts, have coated the seed attached to the cathode and formed the character of the child. The seed, therefore, has been plated with a base metal.

If, on the other hand, a woman knows the laws of gold-plating and decides to apply them in bringing her child into the world then, when a seed is implanted in her womb (cathode), she will put a sheet of gold into her mind (anode), the gold of pure, lofty thoughts. The current is switched on and the blood flowing through her body conveys the precious metal to the seed. The child grows, clothed in gold and turns out to be robust, healthy and beautiful both in physique and in character, and capable of overcoming all difficulties and diseases, all evil influences.

Most mothers have no inkling of the tremendous influence their mental state has on the child in their womb. Later, after it is born, they plan to take care of it and look for suitable people to educate and instruct it. But by then it will be too late; the child will already be set in its mould. No instructor or educator can transform a child who was formed by inferior, perverse elements in its mother's womb; the composition of those elements will not change. If it is dull and lustreless like lead, you can cut and polish it until it shines like silver, but it will always tarnish again very rapidly; that is to say that in spite of an excellent education the child will always revert to its innate weaknesses. I have great faith in the competence of good educators, teachers and pedagogues but, in point of fact, they can do almost nothing. Yes, in spite of the fact that I have a degree in Education and have been director of a college in Bulgaria, I still say this: a good teacher can do a great deal for his pupils, especially in the way of instruction, but he can never change the fundamental nature of those he teaches. He can change a few things but only externally, and that is not enough. If the basic character of a child is flawed, you can give him the best teachers in the world and it will not change anything. Whereas if the child is made of gold, inside, even if he has to live in appalling conditions or in a family of criminals, he will always be good, noble and incorruptible because the essence of his nature is pure. It is absolutely essential that you should know this law.

Mothers have the potential ability to work miracles for the world: it is they who possess the key to the forces of creation. Women could transform the whole of humanity within fifty years, if only they applied the methods of spiritual galvanoplasty. And men must help the women. Even if some women do know what they should do they are prevented from doing it by their ignorant, egotistical and careless husbands. Only when the heart and the intellect, the mother and father, are working as one, will they be able to create a divine child, destined to achieve great things in the world.

Perhaps you are under the impression that women are especially privileged because it is they alone who have the power to transform humanity, but this is not so: every man is also a woman who creates children. His children are his thoughts and feelings. A man is a mother differently from a woman, of course, for his polarity is different, but that does not change the laws : men, too, can apply the methods of galvanoplasty if they become aware of their capabilities.

What is the significance of gold from the point of view of cosmic galvanoplasty? Gold is the perfect matter: pure and enduring. This is why, for centuries, Initiates have always considered gold to be the symbol of the sun. Why do all men love gold and long to possess it? Because it is a crystallization, a concentration of the sun's energies condensed in the earth. Specks of gold are forces, influences flowing from the sun. Gold cannot tarnish. Someone who has a lot of gold in his blood does not succumb to sickness or to the evil influences he encounters in his lifetime; he is safe from misfortune and distress. He who is inwardly poor has a dearth of gold in the blood. Inner gold attracts outer gold. Of course there are some people who are outwardly poor but who are inwardly very rich in virtues, and others who are outwardly wealthy but who are destitute as far as virtue goes. This does not alter the law, it is simply that it applies in different ways.

The phenomenon of galvanoplasty teaches us how to nurture the purest and most noble thoughts and feelings in our minds and hearts in order to bring to full flowering all the qualities our Eternal Father has placed in us since the creation of the world. When we have developed all these qualities to the full we shall resemble our Father; we shall have the visage of perfect love, perfect wisdom and perfect truth. We must work according to the laws of galvanoplasty every day of our lives. Firstly, by implanting in our minds thoughts of durable, incorruptible materials, thoughts of pure gold. Secondly, by carrying constantly, in our heart and soul, the image of some truly exceptional being, Jesus or another great Master. Thirdly, by 'plugging in' to the central powerhouse from which flow all the life-giving forces in the universe. If we do this, as we are immersed in the solution of cosmic ether, all these forces will begin to work in us and accomplish something marvellous. Day by day, subtle particles of matter will flow from our spirit into every part of our body, into every cell, into our face. Under their influence our faces and even our bodies will change until, one day, we shall be a true portrait of love.

We should not let a day go by without thinking about this bond between the sun and the earth, between spirit and matter. Every day we must remember that immense sacrifice the Spirit of God makes for the physical body and which is being consummated every minute of the day and night. This is why we must establish a bond with Heaven, so that this ceaseless stream of energy may flow through us once again. How can we do this? Well, it is very simple. A few moments ago I read you a passage from the Gospel in which Jesus said, 'If two of you agree on earth as touching any thing that they shall ask, it shall be done for them of my Father which is in heaven. For where two or three are gathered together in my name, there am I in the midst of them'. In other words, 'Where the light of the mind, the love of the heart and the activity of the will are, there am I'. The two or three, therefore, must be united. Often, it is enough for two to be united to attract the third to join them. Jesus said 'two or three', not 'four or five'. The two are the one who thinks and the one who desires; the third is the action, the child of the other two. If we want to get results we need only to think and to feel, because action, the fruit of thoughts and feelings, always follows after.

The Gospel text should not be understood literally. When Jesus spoke of 'two or three gathered together in my name', he was not speaking of two or three people. If he had been it would mean that if you found yourself alone in the desert Christ would not be with you because you would be one, not two or three. Or, alternatively, if ten people find themselves together in a railway carriage, they may all be good, honest people but they do not know each other and do not talk to each other. As they are not gathered together in the name of Christ, and as there are ten of them, not two or three, Christ would not be in their midst... You see what conclusions you are forced to come to if you take the Gospels literally! The 'two or three' are the intellect, heart and will. If you understand it this way, then whether you are alone or with a hundred others, Christ will be within you as long as your thoughts and feelings are united in order to accomplish something in his Name. Jesus was saying, in other words, 'Where there is love, wisdom and truth, there am I'.

The current flows between love (the cathode) and wisdom (the anode) and the image attached to the cathode is coated with the metal: this is the activity which is born of the other two and constitutes the third factor. If you eliminate one of the electrodes, one of the poles, the galvanoplastic process necessarily ceases. So you can see why it is so important for the future mother to maintain luminous thoughts in her mind. Thanks to these thoughts the seed that is growing in her, will absorb pure, precious materials and instead of giving birth to a stupid, unhealthy or criminally-minded child, she will bring forth a great artist, a brilliant scholar, a saint, a messenger from God. Her blood, which represents the solution of salts, will convey to the seed all the elements it needs for its nourishment.

If a woman is ignorant of the laws of galvanoplasty and gives free rein to all kinds of weird whims and fancies, entertains shabby thoughts and satisfies all the incoherent cravings she may feel during her pregnancy, she plays into the hands of all those mischievous entities who are plaguing her. In the hope of having some share in the life of the child, later on, these beings try to induce the mother to behave in such a way that the galvanoplasty will be flawed. If they succeed in this, in later years they will be able to go in and out of the child at will, and satisfy their own baser appetites through him.

During the whole period of gestation, whether she is aware of the fact or not, woman's spirit collaborates with the soul that is preparing to incarnate in her child. Some women are sufficiently advanced to be aware of this and even to dialogue consciously with that soul.

Future mothers should be conscious of the tremendous responsibility they assume in bringing a new member of society into existence. It is in their power either to swell the ranks of the crippled and hapless wretches in the world or to give to mankind a saviour who will rid them of their ills. During her pregnancy she must watch over her baby, guarding it from all harmful influences, consciously building up in her mind an atmosphere of purity and light with which to surround it and protect it from attack by malevolent entities. If some children are born to a life of chaos and misery from the beginning, the fault is their mothers'; they were too ignorant and unconscious to do better.

So this is why I launch an appeal to all my sisters, the women of this world: 'Bestir yourselves, my sisters! Wake up to the nobility of the task God has entrusted to you. You have untold secrets in your keeping which must be put to work for the regeneration of humanity, and you're not even aware of their value: you treat them like playthings! You must begin to be conscious of your mission. And your menfolk must try to prepare the best possible conditions in which you may accomplish your immense, magical work.'

Woman is man's mother; man will always be her child. And now, thanks to spiritual galvanoplasty, she must show him what she is capable of. Only one thing is necessary: a high ideal, a sublime ambition. That is all you need. Society has sunk to such depths of moral degradation: disorder, hatred, dishonesty and wars. But women are capable of remedying this state of affairs on condition that they recover the keys they possessed in the past.

If women unite in this sublime ideal of regenerating humanity they will gain the respect of men. Men will be bound, once again to respect and admire them, to appreciate them and seek inspiration from them. Their creative work, their whole attitude will show men the way that leads to sublime heights just as, in the days of old, mothers taught their sons the meaning of true strength, nobility and heroism. In times past it was always woman who educated man. In fact, if I have such deep respect for women and, especially, for mothers, it is due to my own Mother's attitude. My Mother played a very important role in my life. It was she who taught me to love and respect women simply by showing me that no one can be more patient and loving and more willing to accept sacrifices than a mother. Never have I experienced anything comparable to the sublime life of a mother, with the exception, of course, of my Master, Peter Deunov.

The family in which the mother does not rank first, is a lost cause. The society in which the mother does not rank first, degenerates. Don't get the idea that I am saying this because of an exalted imagination or from stupid sentimentality. Not at all: What I am telling you stems from authentic knowledge. And, of course, if I speak of mothers in such glowing terms, it is because I am speaking of the true, ideal mother who gives an example of the most perfect spirit of sacrifice for her children, all her life long.

Hearing what I say about them, many women will probably react, saying: 'That's all very well, but women have been examples of love and kindness for hundreds of years. But men have never understood us: they have always despised us'. Yes, I know. A great many men behave like selfish children, but if they are like that it is because women have never really known how to be mothers. They have never applied the laws of spiritual galvanoplasty while they were carrying their children, so now they are suffering the consequences of their work badly done.

The new era which is just beginning will be the era of love, which means that it will be the era of woman. At the moment women have gone considerably astray: They even attempt to outdo men in their shamelessness, licentiousness and frivolity. They fancy that in this way they can revenge themselves for all those years when they led restricted lives and were not free to do as they liked. But they do not realize that that kind of behaviour will inevitably lead to catastrophe. If there is still some goodness left in woman let her immediately do whatever she can to preserve it in order to save the human race. This evening, for the first time, I make this appeal to all the women in the world: 'Meditate on spiritual galvanoplasty! If you live your nine months of pregnancy unconsciously and in the midst of disorder, you will have to put up with the consequences for the rest of your lives: you will be assailed by disappointment, conflict and misunderstandings. Whereas if you accomplish your task consciously and wisely your reward will be everlasting; you will be the mother-goddess and an inspiration for generations of human beings'.

At present, neither men nor women are aware of these laws. Not only do they not choose the moment when their child will be conceived, more often than not, when that time comes, the man acts with violence and passion; sometimes, even, he is drunk... he behaves like an animal. In doing violence to his wife, he provokes negative reactions on her part, she begins to entertain feelings of revenge and hatred, contempt or disgust. No wonder then, that in these conditions, there are so many criminals, freaks and degenerates, and so few who are capable of working for good. Mankind is sinking ever further into obscurity and one of the reasons for this is the prevailing ignorance about the laws of spiritual galvanoplasty.

Let me tell you a very interesting anecdote about Alexander the Great. There is a tradition that, when he was a young boy, Alexander loved to go and visit an astrologer who lived quite near the royal palace. This astrologer was very knowledgeable and he worked in a room at the top of a high tower from which he could observe the movements of the stars, the aspects of the planets and so on. One day, when Alexander was with the astrologer he suddenly asked him if he knew when he would die. 'Yes, my child', said the old man, 'I know.' 'And do you know how you'll die?' asked Alexander, 'If so, tell me.' 'My own son will kill me', said the astrologer. 'What nonsense!' exclaimed Alexander, 'You have no wife or children, and now you're too old to have any. So take that...' Suddenly Alexander, who was very impulsive, gave the old man a push and toppled him off the top of the tower. Racing down the steps and out of the tower, he found the old astrologer lying on the ground, dying. Bending over him, Alexander said, 'You see? You said you would be killed by your son, but it wasn't your son who killed you : it was me!' With his dying breath the astrologer answered, 'Yes, it is truly my son who has killed me, for you are my son. Ask your mother... the stars don't lie'. At that moment Alexander understood why his mother visited the astrologer so often. He bitterly repented what he had done and insisted that his father be buried with due honours.

Now I have not told you this story so that the women should all go looking for astrologers to father their children, but Alexander the Great is a good example of how astrology can help us to have children who will turn out to be exceptional human beings. The astrologer and the Queen had calculated the exact moment for the conception so that the child would be born under favourable aspects. Conception took place in the last few days of August, (with the Sun in Leo and very powerful), because the astrologer's calculations showed that this would bring the child to the moment of birth with the Sun in Aries (in which it is exalted) and Jupiter in a favourable aspect with Mars. In addition, the Sun was very close to the meridian, in the tenth house, while Leo was in the first house with Jupiter and Mars in trine with the Sun. All this indicated extremely favourable conditions for power, wealth and worldly glory. Saturn, on the other hand, was negatively aspected with the Sun.

Obviously, the astrologer must have calculated the child's horoscope in relation to his·own, but the problem is that one cannot always know for certain just how long a child will remain in its mother's womb. One can calculate the date of birth to within a few days and know approximately where the planets will be in relation to the Zodiac and the aspects between them, but the child can be born a few days early or a few days late. It was only after Alexander was born that his father, the astrologer, could compare the two horoscopes and see that he would be killed by his own son.

Certain occultists see a similitude in the horoscopes of Alexander the Great and Napoleon, who was born when the Sun was in Leo with Jupiter in the first house; they think that the same spirit incarnated in the two of them. It is an interesting idea, but we shall not spend time on that today.

Let's go back to galvanoplasty.

We sometimes complain that God is cruel and unjust or that He does not love us, but it is simply because we are not just in our own minds. We are under the impression that we deserve happiness and success and then, when some misfortune overtakes us, we think that Heaven has sent us this for no reason. We forget that, every day, God gives us the possibility of hearing, feeling, seeing, breathing, walking about... and even of indulging in every form of madness we are capable of inventing! The disastrous result of this attitude is that the galvanoplastic process comes to a stop. When someone is incapable of giving thanks, of being grateful to God, Nature and Heaven, the vital process of galvanoplasty is interrupted.

It is as though he had thrown a switch on the main pow-erline: the current that brings strength and blessings from on high can no longer get through to him; the forces of creative life no longer flow within him.

We should never let a day go by without thinking of our colossal indebtedness to God... otherwise we shall lose all we have. If we do not appreciate health, we shall fall ill. If we are not grateful for our sense of hearing we shall become deaf, and so on. And when we have lost one of these treasures we shall begin to appreciate it in earnest.

Look at all the extraordinary wealth we possess without realizing it: our hearts, intellects and wills. The greatest Initiates needed nothing more: they made all their discoveries with no other instruments than these. We are capable of any-thing if we use them correctly, but, of course, it takes more than a few days. Our capabilities increase progressively as we use what we have received and if we work patiently, one day we shall reap the fruits of our labours.

The phenomenon of galvanoplasty can be applied in so many different areas that it would be impossible to reveal everything in one evening. So let me just repeat that we are immersed in a cosmic solution and that we have to connect our two electrodes to the two poles of the battery – God – and switch on the current. At the moment, wherever one turns, one sees that the electrodes are disconnected: in families (be-cause the father and mother do not get along well), in our-selves (our hearts and intellects pull in opposite directions), in society and in the world community, etc. And how can one recognize the rupture between our electrodes? Well, for one thing, we have magnificent ideas but the way we live is con-stantly in contradiction to our ideas; we talk about Angels and Initiates, but we continue to wrong our neighbour, we continue to be demanding, egotistical and prideful. Everyone considers this dichotomy between our thoughts, feelings and actions natural. No, it is not natural!

If someone gazes constantly at the same image, the phenomenon of galvanoplasty will apply so that he will become more and more like the object of his contemplation. You all know that people who live together for a long time and who love each other and think about each other, end by looking alike. In fact one can often see a striking resemblance between some animals and their masters. Sometimes it is the dog who gets to look like its master but sometimes, unfortunately, it is the master who begins to look like his dog!

There exist certain laws, therefore, which we can use to advance our evolution. If you have understood what I have told you, you will start putting it into practice at once, this very evening. Choose the image of a beautiful, pure, strong, wise being, full of love; place that image in your spirit and contemplate it in a spirit of adoration. In this way you set an electric current flowing which will convey to your heart the noblest particles in solution in your blood, and your countenance will reflect more and more faithfully the object of your contemplation.

Perhaps you think it is difficult to achieve this just by looking at an image. That is true. It is difficult; it cannot be done in a day or even in a week, but if you persevere in patience and faith, you will see results. At the moment you still have horrible images within you which keep you chained to inferior states of mind: you must change them.

Place in your hearts the image of a Master, of Christ or a great Initiate and let it be your 'sweetheart', for love is the primordial force which leads to exchanges.

Lyon, June 9, 1938

11

The Mother's Role
During Gestation

Adults have more and more complaints about the misdeeds of the young: they do not want to work any more, they refuse to obey, they are constantly in a state of rebellion because they want to be free to do as they please, etc. All that is true. In fact it is reaching alarming proportions: there have never been so many crimes, so many thefts, and when women and girls are attacked in the streets it is usually by young people. What can be done to remedy all that?

So many things exist for the instruction of mankind: radio and television, newspapers, books and universities, and people imagine that all this will make things better. Not at all! To instruct men is to arm them. As long as one is content to give people more and more information without attempting to change anything on the inside, instruction is dangerous, for men use it simply to satisfy their passions and their basest desires. From time to time, someone explains that it is not good

* For the last thirty-five years Master Omraam Mikhaël Aïvanhov has constantly talked about spiritual galvanoplasty so it seems appropriate to add these few pages from a more recent lecture. (Editor's note)

to live without respect for moral law, but that is not enough. In that case, what can one do to improve humanity? Today I shall tell you just a little about the solution I have in mind : another day I shall talk about it in greater detail.

The regeneration of humanity is possible only on condition that we take care of the children... even before their birth : in other words, if we take care of pregnant women. It is not necessary to know about everything that is going on in the world in order to improve man's destiny : all we need to know are the true laws of Creation, for everything is based on those laws. We have to begin at the roots, therefore, and if the way in which children are born can be improved, within a few years the whole human race will be improved. Whereas, if men are left with all their weaknesses, I assure you, whatever one gives them they will manage to use it for their own self-interest, to further their ambition and satisfy their vanity and their lower instincts. Children must be formed, therefore, before birth, by taking care of their mothers for, during pregnancy, a woman has a great deal of power over her child. Once it is born it is too late ; the child escapes her.

In the hope of improving the national and international situation, all kinds of plans are elaborated : political, financial, economic, military ; it is amazing how many brilliant ideas the planners have. One cannot help but be lost in admiration ! The only trouble is that none of these plans has ever done much good because they all concentrate on purely material aspects : technological progress, increased production, more laboratories and universities, increasing or diminishing arms, etc... and human beings are still in the same predicament : still in the same state of disorder, unhappiness and revolt. So, in view of the situation I have decided to offer my own plan. Perhaps you will say, 'What vanity ! What presumptuousness !' Perhaps, but if someone can produce a use-

ful, effective plan, surely he has the right to do so? You too...
But you will soon see: my plan is extremely simple.

Instead of spending billions and billions on hospitals, prisons, magistrates, schools, I would advise the State to take care, only, of its pregnant women: the cost would be far less and the results would be far better. I would ask the government to acquire several hundred acres that I would choose in a very beautiful, well orientated area of the country and to plan an estate there. There would have to be residences, for which I would give some indications as to style and colours, etc., and they would be embellished with paintings and sculptures and so on. There would be parks and gardens, also, with all kinds of trees and flowers. This is where the future mothers would live during their pregnancy. The cost of their food and lodging would be borne by the State. They would spend their nine months in these beautiful, poetic surroundings, going for walks, listening to music and attending lectures about how to live the period of gestation: what to eat, of course, but also and more important, how to work by means of their thoughts and feelings on the child in their womb. Their husbands would be allowed to visit them and they, too, would have to learn how to behave towards their wives. In this way, in conditions of peace and quiet and beauty, women would bring children into the world who would be fit channels for all manner of heavenly blessings.

Whereas, as things stand at present, amongst all the spirits who incarnate these days, only a handful comes from Heaven. All the others come straight from Hell. This is because the doors are closed to heavenly spirits: they cannot incarnate in bodies that have been prepared in conditions of evil and chaos. And this is why the human race is not getting any better. It is possible for it to improve, of course, through great suffering, but that is a route that takes thousands of years. If we do as I have described, the human race would improve very rapidly and without being obliged to take the path of suffering and disaster. But the very first thing you must understand is that all the attempts that have been made so far to improve humanity by changing material, economic policies, have never achieved their purpose: humanity is still mired in the same passions, the same vices... in fact it is perhaps worse than ever! And yet the human race can be improved, but on this one condition: that one begin at the beginning, that is with mothers.

If you only knew what intolerable conditions many pregnant women have to put up with! They live in cramped, dark slums, they bear all the burdens of the family. And on top of all that, when a man comes home drunk or in a state of frustration and rage because he cannot find work or has been abused by a comrade, he will often vent his anger on his wife, abusing and even beating her. In these conditions how can you expect her to produce a genius? That is why, instead of building maternity hospitals, it would be far better to spend the money on giving mothers the ideal conditions for bearing children. Afterwards, if they have to, they can go back to their slums; their children will build them palaces. It is the children who will rescue the parents from their misery, because they will be talented and capable people.

As it is – and the situation is getting worse – women are giving birth to worthless, sick, unbalanced children and then, of all stupid things! they send them to school or to the doctor or even to correctional institutions in the hope of reforming or transforming or educating them. The fact of the matter is that the original quintessence provided by the mother at the very beginning can never be altered or improved. Even if one continues to spend billions on so-called improvements in psychological or pedagogical methods, it will be no use. Whereas, with the method I propose, in forty or fifty years things would change: the world would be peopled by honest, intelligent men and women and, even, many saints, geniuses and Initiates.

Oh, yes. I know: they will say that my ideas are not scientific. For my part, I think they are just as scientific, in fact more so, than what other people propose. No one has the right to criticize my plan without trying it first. I must, of course, warn you that the situation will not be righted absolutely overnight: several generations will be needed, for parents have their own heritage of weakness and vice which will do its best to slip into their children. But if the parents of today are careful there will be a real improvement in only one generation. Of course there will be a few defective elements that manage to slip in because the parents will not all be able to purify themselves completely. But the second generation will be better, and the third better still and, little by little, all the impurities of the past will disappear.

If intelligent people in positions of influence would just think about this and take it seriously, they would understand – for it can be explained scientifically and in detail – what goes on in an expectant mother and how – on condition that she understands the laws of galvanoplasty, that she be cared for with affection and that she be helped by adequate material conditions – she has the power not only to fashion the physical body, but also the mental and astral bodies of her child out of the best possible materials and elements.

Unfortunately, I know in advance that my plan will be rejected, that no one will give it really serious consideration, because the present generation has been so well moulded and fashioned by other philosophies that there is no room in their heads for these ideas. Even the most advanced medical research is not prepared to recognize these truths. Recently a sister of our Brotherhood was in a maternity home to have her baby and while talking to the doctor, one day, she told him she belonged to a spiritual Teaching which revealed how the mother could influence her baby by her thoughts. And do you know how the doctor replied? He roared with laughter, saying, 'Don't you believe it! What idiotic ideas. How can a mother's ideas possibly change anything?' You see what doctors know about it! And to think that people expect to be enlightened by people like that...

I am not particularly up to date as far as my knowledge of scientific research goes, but I know that some biologists, experimenting with mice, have discovered that fear and anxiety in a pregnant mouse can affect the young. So they came to the conclusion that there was a link between the mother and the child during gestation. When I heard that, I thought to myself, 'There we are. Now we shall hear the truth.' But at the same time I was furious. Instead of applauding this great discovery I was very angry! Why, instead of studying mice and putting all one's faith in mice, don't they study women who have been having babies for thousands of years? I hope biologists will forgive me, but it is sheer stupidity! They don't study women, they study mice. Is it to be mice who will teach human beings what is true and what is false? They have built laboratories for mice and are convinced that they are fantastically important, whereas they don't give a second thought to the laboratories that nature created millions of years ago and which are far better equipped than those built by human beings. How can one help but be indignant at such reasoning? For more than thirty-five years I have been explaining that a woman's state of mind reflects on the child in her womb. I gave a lecture about galvanoplasty in which I showed how this phenomenon is to be found in the spiritual life and in the process of gestation. But that was not good enough: the world was waiting for the mice to declare themselves! Now mice are to be the teachers of humanity. And what about women? The whole thing is extremely insulting for them! How can they help being indignant? I advise all women to rebel against the situation: parade through the streets with banners; hold meetings. Just wait and see: I will yet manage to sow the seeds of revolt amongst women!

As for me, I leave the mice in peace. I have observed women who are pregnant and, a few years later, I have observed their children, and I have seen that the worries and difficulties the mother experienced at certain moments of her pregnancy were reflected in the corresponding periods in the life of the child. But mankind was waiting to be enlightened by mice... and in the meantime the world has been peopled by monsters. Even if biologists have, at last, understood, they are still very behindhand : if humanity is going to have to wait to be educated by them, they are going to have to wait a long time; their methods are so slow. But in any case, there is not much chance that they will do anything to help women : all they are interested in is mice.

We have to go back to the beginning : man who creates himself. Once he is created, if he turns out to be deformed, you can give him whatever you like, put him in the best possible conditions, send him to the best possible schools or universities, it is too late. Look at a production line in a factory : if a part is defective, do they try to mend it or patch it up? Not a bit of it : they send it back to be melted down and recast. When it comes to producing material objects in a factory men go about it intelligently, but when it is a question of making children their common sense abandons them. Everyone knows that a specific kind of seed will produce the same kind of plant, and an egg will produce only its own species of animal, but no one applies these laws to human beings : they plant thistles and are then disappointed at not being able to harvest figs !

It is obvious, isn't it? It is the parents who need education. Of course, parents will say, 'What do you mean? We are giving our children a good example'. Yes, perhaps this is true externally, but how do you behave when you are alone? That's the point. People count far too much on the visible form or appearances : clothes, facial expressions, gestures, and on that score they pass muster, but on the inside, all kinds of weird things are going on. That is why I talked to you, one day, about Nature's memory: how everything we do is recorded in our chromosomes. Every cell in the body has a memory, so even if someone acts a part and pretends to be friendly, honest and charitable with others, it is his innermost thoughts and feelings that are recorded and it is these that are handed down from generation to generation. And if the parents' chromosomes bear a record of weaknesses, disease and vice, once these have been passed on to the child, you can go looking for specialized teachers, schools or doctors: it will not do you a bit of good. It is too late. Everything gets handed on and if it does not surface in the first generation it will do so in the second or third. Human beings have to understand that nature is honest and faithful. The proverb says, 'He who sows the wind shall reap the whirlwind'. The great laws of nature are not to be trifled with. Everything is subject to improvement but only if Divine Intelligence is our guide. And we are capable of knowing Divine Intelligence: it has been revealed to us, it is within us. It is up to us, now, to align ourselves more and more closely with these divine laws and to understand that everything is reflected and recorded within us.

Men never go to the roots, the causes of things; they are only interested in the consequences. Recently, someone gave me one of those little wooden houses that act as a barometer: the house is divided into two parts, on one side there is a little man with a hat, and on the other a little old lady with an umbrella. When the man comes out of the house the weather is fine, and when the woman comes out, the weather changes and it begins to rain. What conclusion do we draw from that? That it is the little old lady who decides what the weather is going to be like? You may well laugh, but almost everybody reasons like that! They worry about the consequences instead of worrying about the causes and they think they can improve things by remedying the consequences. But they never improve anything because, if you do not touch the causes they will continue to produce the same disastrous results. Take just one example: the problem of mosquitos. You kill the mosquitos but do nothing to get rid of the swamps in which they breed. I am not talking about physical swamps: everyone knows they have to be dried out. I am talking about spiritual swamps: it is in that area that people let the causes continue to produce their noxious effects. They attempt to remedy these effects, for example, by sending people to hospital or to asylums, to prison and even to the gallows, but no one tries to do anything about the cause: the way in which children are brought into this world and the way they are formed in their mothers' womb. You must get back to the cause. Have you understood that?

As long as those who want to instruct their fellow men and remedy the ills of society do not know true Initiatic Science, disease and human suffering will continue. Whatever political system. is adopted, whatever social transformations are achieved, the basic situation will remain unchanged. As the French say: 'Plus ça change plus c'est la même chose' (The more things change the more they stay the same). I have already told you: it is instruction that makes people so individualistic and anarchistic. As soon as people get a little information in their heads they begin to revolt and take up arms: this is the result of instruction. I am not saying that people should not be taught, but they must be taught something different, something that will not inevitably lead to disaster. The instruction young people receive today contains none of the elements it needs to turn them into noble, generous, disinterested men and women. On the contrary, it arouses all their worst instincts of lust, ambition and revolt.

Of course, even when children have been properly formed in the womb they will still need some form of instruction but it should not come first in importance: only third or fourth. At the moment, not only is it considered all-important, but it crams the youngsters' heads with information that leaves their souls and spirits untouched and which totally ignores the divine dimension, the Creator. People will tell you : 'That's the Church's business'; but that is not true. A true educator must, first and foremost, awaken young people to another world, with all its laws and structures and inner organisation. Once they have this you can safely leave them to themselves ! Their awareness of this other world will be constantly active in them and will guide them : they will never turn out to be anarchistic, idle, insubordinate or criminally minded. In a previous lecture, I talked to you about how a mother can work in collaboration with the soul of her future baby. The soul enters a child's body as soon as it draws its first breath but it takes a long time for it to gain control of all the organs. In fact, even when the child is born, the soul does not completely enter its body; some part of it still stays outside. Nevertheless, the mother can communicate with the future soul of her baby during the period of gestation. She may not see it but she can promise to do her part and ask the soul to be generous : 'I will do my best to contribute the best possible materials. I will help you in your work, but please do your best to contribute such and such a quality so that my child may be an artist... a philosopher... a scholar or a saint.' And during the whole of that period she must take care about her behaviour and not let herself be led astray by unreasonable urges and sudden cravings – for a woman becomes extremely sensitive and impressionable during pregnancy – because all these irregularities will be reflected in her baby.

Our Teaching also explains how men and women should prepare to conceive a child, what their state of mind should be, how important it is for them to be pure. Even before conception future fathers and mothers should be prepared for their role; they must learn how to love, how to go about their exchange in such a way as to ensure the aid of cosmic Intelligences and the presence of Angels. But don't delude yourselves: most people are very far from such preoccupations! They wait until they are drunk or have lost control of themselves: it is then that most children are conceived.

The key to the whole question is in the hands of women; it is they who are capable of transforming the human race. If they listen to me and understand, they will become such an irresistible force in the world, nothing will be able to stand up to them. Women must understand what I am saying and unite to achieve this tremendous ideal. At the moment they are disunited except in one thing: their readiness to seduce men and lure them into their snares, and this is why they are not really a force to be reckoned with yet. The time has come for women to leave all their petty pleasures, their absorption in make-up and clothes, and unite in the determination to regenerate humanity. So often, even during pregnancy, they live heedlessly and spend all their time on futile nothings. They seem to think that all they need do is to find teachers and doctors, later on, to look after their child and heal and instruct it. Don't you believe it! No educator and no doctor can ever change the underlying nature of a child. Perhaps they can apply a little superficial polish, but nothing more. All the improvements attempted in later years will not touch the child's character: they will simply be a kind of domestication. It is exactly the same as with savages: you can give them a little superficial education and teach them how to dress and have decent table manners, but it will not last: as soon as they are back in their tribal setting they revert to type. Whether a man be a criminal or a saint, nobody will ever change the fact of what he is. He can, perhaps, be influenced superficially and temporarily, but deep down in himself he will not be changed.

The possibility exists, thanks to the power that nature has given to women, for the world to be peopled, one day, with wonderful, healthy, good and intelligent men and women. Nature has given women powers which they have not begun to exploit to the full, or which they exploit for the wrong purposes. They must be made aware of their potential, and they must realize that the future of the whole human race is in their hands. In spite of their intelligence and all their skills, men cannot do very much in this area. It is the mother, woman, who is preordained by Nature to fashion the child in the womb.

In the hope of enlightening and liberating women, I want to say this to them: 'Are you still wasting your time on trivialities? For Goodness' sake, wake up! Reclaim the place God has assigned to you from the beginning of the world... It is you who have to regenerate humanity: the task is a glorious one and only you can do it.' And I would ask the sisters in this Teaching to have it at heart, at the very least, to enlighten all their sisters throughout the world who still know nothing of all this. I promise you that this ideal, the desire to be useful, will fill your hearts and souls and spirits to overflowing. You will never want for inspiration or gladness, you will always feel rich, for this ideal of contributing to the happiness of mankind will sustain and nourish you. Nothing will ever satisfy you if you do not cherish this ideal in your soul. Whatever else you may possess you will always be in the same state of dissatisfaction and inner void. Whereas if you are fired with the ideal of fulfilling your God-given mission and doing what Heaven expects of you, you will always be radiant, full of gladness and light.

May light and peace be with you!

Le Bonfin, July 20, 1969

By the same author
(translated from the French)

'Complete Works' Collection

Volume 1 – The Second Birth
Volume 2 – Spiritual Alchemy
Volume 5 – Life Force
Volume 6 – Harmony
Volume 7 – The Mysteries of Yesod
Volume 10 – The Splendour of Tiphareth
Volume 11 – The Key to the Problems of Existence
Volume 12 – Cosmic Moral Laws
Volume 13 – A New Earth
             Methods, Exercises, Formulas, Prayers
Volume 14 – Love and Sexuality (Part I)
Volume 15 – Love and Sexuality (Part II)
Volume 25 – Aquarius, Herald of the Golden Age (Part I)
Volume 26 – Aquarius, Herald of the Golden Age (Part II)
Volume 29 – On the Art of Teaching (Part III)
Volume 32 – The Fruits of the Tree of Life
             The Cabbalistic Tradition

Brochures :

New Presentation

301 – The New Year
302 – Meditation
303 – Respiration
304 – Death and the Life Beyond

By the same author :
(translated from the French)

Izvor Collection

201 – Toward a Solar Civilization
202 – Man, Master of his Destiny
203 – Education Begins Before Birth
204 – The Yoga of Nutrition
205 – Sexual Force or the Winged Dragon
206 – A Philosophy of Universality
207 – What is a Spiritual Master ?
208 – The Egregor of the Dove or the Reign of Peace
209 – Christmas and Easter in the Initiatic Tradition
210 – The Tree of the Knowledge of Good and Evil
211 – Freedom, the Spirit Triumphant
212 – Light is a Living Spirit
213 – Man's Two Natures : Human and Divine
214 – Hope for the World : Spiritual Galvanoplasty
215 – The True Meaning of Christ's Teaching
216 – The Living Book of Nature
217 – New Light on the Gospels
218 – The Symbolic Language of Geometrical Figures
219 – Man's Subtle Bodies and Centres
220 – The Zodiac, Key to Man and to the Universe
221 – True Alchemy or the Quest for Perfection
222 – Man's Psychic Life : Elements and Structures
223 – Creation : Artistic and Spiritual
224 – The Powers of Thought
225 – Harmony and Health
226 – The Book of Divine Magic
228 – Looking into the Invisible

PRINTED IN FRANCE IN SEPTEMBER 1989
EDITIONS PROSVETA, Z.I. DU CAPITOU – B.P.12
83601 FRÉJUS CEDEX
FRANCE

– N° d'impression : 1757 –
Dépôt légal : Septembre 1989
Printed in France